LITTLE-KNOWN MUSEUMS
IN AND AROUND
ROME

LITTLE-KNOWN MUSEUMS IN AND AROUND ROME

by Rachel Kaplan

HARRY N. ABRAMS, INC., PUBLISHERS

This book is for Adele, my editor, my mentor, my friend.

Editor: Adele Westbrook
Designer: Lorraine Ferguson

Library of Congress Cataloging-in-Publication Data
Kaplan, Rachel.
  Little-known museums in and around Rome / by Rachel Kaplan.
    p. cm.
  Includes bibliographical references and index.
  ISBN 0-8109-2914-7
  1. Museums—Italy—Rome—Guidebooks. 2. Rome (Italy)—Guidebooks. I. Title.

  AM55.R6 K36 2000
  069'.09421—dc21   00–20535

Front cover:
The Pleasure Casino and Fountains of the Palazzo Farnese at Caprarola in Viterbo.

Back cover:
The laurel-crowned head of Napoleon, representing him as a Roman Senator,
dominates the entrance to the Napoleonic Museum in Rome.

Rachel Kaplan was educated at the Lycée Français de New York and at Northwestern
University, where she earned a B.S. in Journalism. She is an international correspondent
who has written articles for American, British, French, and Czech publications on
a wide range of subjects. She is the author of *Little-Known Museums In and Around
Paris*, *Little-Known Museums In and Around London*, and *Little-Known Museums
In and Around Berlin*, as well as the co-author of *A La Découverte des Plus Belles
Routes Ile-de-France*. She is also the president of French Links, a cultural tourism
company based in Paris.

Printed and bound in Hong Kong

Harry N. Abrams, Inc.
100 Fifth Avenue
New York, N.Y. 10011
www.abramsbooks.com

CONTENTS

———◆———

Acknowledgments

◆

A stone's throw from the Palatine Bridge lies the fabled Tempio della Fortuna Virile (Temple of Human Fortune), one of the best preserved temples in Rome, dating from the late second century B.C. Judging by my adventures in developing this book, I not only believe the Goddess of Human Fortune was working overtime, but that she brought me good luck almost everywhere I ventured.

First, I was given the golden opportunity to begin examining the feasibility of this project while a guest at the American Academy in Rome—a place which every writer and scholar hopes will be duplicated in Heaven. For this I must thank its Executive Director, Wayne Linker, who kindly invited me to stay in the Gisela Richter apartment and make ample use of the Academy's outstanding research library. It was in this very library that I discovered a book that would prove indispensable while exploring the manifold riches of the Eternal City: Georgina Masson's delightfully informative *The Companion Guide to Rome*. Imagine my surprise when I learned that she had written her book in the American Academy's library!

Fate had other surprises in store for me, as well. When I found myself caught in a transportation strike, and hadn't the faintest idea how I was going to make my way around the city, a very welcoming Roman, Dr. Celestino Spada, took me under his wing. Upon telling him that I was working on an illustrated volume on the little-known museums of Rome, he assured me with great confidence that he knew just *the* photographer for such an ambitious project! That is how I met the talented and dedicated Giovanna Piemonte, who is responsible for almost all the color and black-and-white illustrations in this book. Giovanna brought special insight and sensitivity to this project, partly because of her personal association with Rome's museums. (Her grandfather, Felice Barnabei, the noted Italian archaeologist, founded the Etruscan Museum at the Villa Giulia, which is featured in this book.) She once told me: "You have to know how to look at a work of art before you can photograph it." The splendid photographs in this volume, which were produced in record time, prove her point. But unlike some photographers, who may only be comfortable following a shooting script, Giovanna made a wider contribution—going out of her way to supply valuable information about different works of art, and assisting in the final selection of the thirty museums in this volume. Thanks to her, I discovered the Burcardo Theater Museum, the Permanent Exhibition of Carriages, the Giorgio de Chirico Museum, the Jewish Museum of Rome, the Ceramic Museum in the Brugiotti Palace, and the Umberto Mastroianni Museum. In addition, I would like to thank Gianluca Bianchi, a very talented and dedicated assistant photographer, who also helped bring this book to fruition.

It is possible that illustrating this book might have proved an overwhelming task had Giovanna not recommended that we work in tandem with Adele "Dedy" Clerici, a seasoned arts and culture editor for such Italian publications as *Audrey* and *Rivista della Nazione*. Highly organized and determined to pull off an "Italian miracle," Adele took on a staggering amount of the paperwork that was necessary in order to photograph each of these museums. Obtaining these vital permissions proved all the more challenging during the year before the Jubilee, when half of Rome was under scaffolding, and many museums were closed for repairs and renovation. Under such circumstances, it seems only right to mention with gratitude the warm and generous welcome that I received from the Natale family, owners and managers of the much beloved Hotel Navona, five minutes away from the Corso Vittorio Emanuele and Piazza Navona.

Being the beneficiaries and custodians of some of the world's greatest art is no easy task for any museum director or curator, least of all in Rome. All whom I met deserve to be congratulated for their dedication, passion, and scholarship, as well as their fortitude in the midst of urban and political flux. I want to personally thank them all for their assistance in developing *Little-Known Museums In and Around Rome*: Dott.ssa Emilia Talamo, Art Center ACEA-Centrale, Montemartini; Dott.ssa Nicoletta Pagliardi, Direttrice, Aula Ottagona nelle Terme di Diocleziano; Prof. Riondino, Resp. Sovrintendente, Casino del Bel Respiro; Principessa Claudia Ruspoli, Castello Ruspoli; Dr. Sivigliano Alloisi, Galleria Corsini d'Arte Antica a Palazzo Corsini; Prince Jonathan Pamphilj, Direttore, Galleria Doria Pamphilj; Romoli Appolloni, Direttore, Mostra Permanente di Carrozze; Dott.ssa Benedetta Adembri, Museo Archeologico Nazionale Di

Palestrina; Dott.ssa Donatella Mazzeo, Direttrice, Museo Nazionale di Arte Orientale; Dott.ssa Maria Teresa Nota, Direttrice, Museo Barracco; Dott.ssa Maria Teresa Iovinelli, Museo del Burcardo; Dott.ssa Patrizia Rozzi, Museo della Casina delle Civette; Dott.ssa Francesca Riccio, Direttrice, Museo della Ceramica, Palazzo Brugiotti; Dott.ssa Claudia Greco, Direttrice di Ministero di Grazia e Giustizia, Dipartimento dell' Amministrazione Penitenziaria, Dott.ssa Assunta Borzacchiello, Museo Criminilogico di Roma; Dr. Lorenzo Zichichi, Museo Donazione Umberto Mastroianni; Dott.ssa Anna Ascarelli Bleyer, Direttrice, Museo Ebraico di Roma; Inge Manzù, Dott.ssa Livia Velani, Direttrice, Museo Giacomo Manzù-Ardea; Prof. Paolo Picozza, Presidente della Fondazione, Museo Giorgio De Chirico; Dott.ssa Patrizia Rosazza, Direttrice, Museo Mario Praz; Dott.ssa Marina Sapelli, Direttrice, Dott.ssa Rosanna Frigeri, Palazzo Massimo alle Terme-Museo Nazionale Romano; Dott.ssa Giulia Gorgoni, Dr. Giuseppe Castelli, Museo Napoleonico; Dott.ssa Giulia Boetto, Museo delle Navi Romane di Fiumicino; Dott.ssa Francesca Boitani, Direttrice, Museo Nazionale Etrusco di Villa Giulia; Mao Benedetti, Sveva Di Martino, Museo dell' Olio della Sabina; Alfredo Rinaldi, 85th QM-5th Army WWII Vets Honorary Member, Museo dello Sbarco di Anzio; Dott.ssa Matilde De Angelis D'Ossat, Direttrice, Palazzo Altemps-Museo Nazionale Roma; Dott.ssa Rosalba Cantone, Direttrice, Palazzo Farnese a Caprarola; Dott.ssa Maria Lucrezia Vicini, Direttrice, Palazzo I Galleria Spada; Prof. Rodolfo

Donzelli, C.A. Conservatore, Villa Farnesina; Dott.ssa Simona Olivetti, Villa Madama. (Special thanks also goes to the cultural association Citta Nascosta, which organizes tours to places with limited access, including Villa Madama and Casino del Bel Respiro; they were very helpful in the preparation of this book.)

I will never tire of expressing my gratitude to Paul Gottlieb, President and Editorial Director of Harry N. Abrams, Inc., who has believed in the value and importance of the *Little-Known Museums* series from its very inception. Not only has he been adamant about maintaining the quality of this series, but he has also shown me great personal generosity and commitment. Everyone who cares about books knows that Paul Gottlieb and his hardworking team have made Harry N. Abrams, Inc., the most respected illustrated book publisher in the world today.

My editor, Adele Westbrook, has been a godsend. While she has retained my voice and vision throughout this Series, she has always made sure that each one of the four volumes would be beautifully written and handsomely produced. She is a perfectionist, and I love her for this, and for so much more besides. I am so fortunate to have had the privilege of working with her, and of learning from her, every step of the way. I also want to reiterate my admiration for Lorraine Ferguson, who established this Series' design. And I want to thank the lively and original Carol Morgan, who has helped to bring these books to the attention of the public.

On a more personal note, I want to thank my soul mate Alexandre, who has encouraged and supported me during the entire development of the *Little-Known Museums* Series, even if it meant my being absent for weeks at a time. He has understood my passion for learning, and has sustained it in countless ways. Every writer should be so lucky.

—R.K.

Introduction

For the past seven hundred years, since Pope Boniface VIII proclaimed 1300 as Year of Jubilee (the first Holy Year) with plenary indulgences for pilgrims at the Apostles' shrines, visitors have been coming to Rome in record numbers. Even with the dangers that could be encountered along the way and the limited means of transportation, more than two million pilgrims arrived for that first Jubilee, since it had been rumored that anyone who visited St. Peter's would receive total absolution for their sins.

Guides written specifically for these travelers to Rome proposed various tours. One of the oldest and most famous, dating from the eighth or ninth century, and known as the *Einsiedeln Itinerary* (because the man-uscript was found in the Einsiedeln Monastery in Switzerland), offered pilgrims eleven walks through the city. The guide gave a detailed description of the city walls, enumerating the towers, crenellations, windows, and even latrines. It also placed special emphasis on inscriptions—texts that the ancients had engraved on monu-ments—an important field in the renewal of classical studies.

The Renaissance brought new types of visitors to Rome—admirers of Antiquity and amateurs in the study of art. Humanist scholars who were familiar with the ancient Roman authors were more and more interested in the city's architectural heritage, which they wished to study and protect from future harm. By 1462, the city's public authorities had already issued an edict intended to prevent further vandalism of the ancient monuments. This was a radical turnaround from the early years of Christianity, when it was considered a pious duty to smash any pagan statue. (It is partly for this reason that so little original Greek statuary is left in existence.) Less than a decade later, on January 18, 1471, Pope Sixtus IV opened to the public the first large collection of antiquities in the Palazzo dei Conservatori on the Capitoline Hill.

Unlike other cities in Europe, Rome's museums and art collections were assembled essentially by the Popes (the Vatican holds the greatest collection of antique sculptures in the world), and the familial dynasties that benefited from their election, including the Colonna, the Corsini, the Farnese, the Pamphilj, and the Spada families. Thanks to this papal munificence, from the Renaissance until the end of the seventeenth century, Rome was the center of artistic patronage, which is why it became such a mecca for for-eign artists such as Murillo, Velázquez, Poussin, and Rubens.

What is particularly compelling about a visit to Rome, is to find that not only is it the world's largest outdoor museum, known for both its ancient ruins and splendid Baroque churches, but also that many of its riches are still tucked away in palaces that were built during the Renaissance and Baroque periods. Yet, unlike Paris, London, or New York, Rome has no major museum covering all the arts, such as the Louvre, the National Gallery, or the Metropolitan Museum of Art.

Within the past five years, the open-ing of several new museums, including the Palazzo Altemps, the ACEA Art Center at the Montemartini Power

Station, the Giorgio De Chirico Museum, the Burcardo Theater Museum, the Umberto Mastroianni Museum, and the Museum of the Swiss Cottage of the Owls, demonstrates that the city is responding to new public interests and a heightened influx of tourists that has increased twenty-five percent in the last five years.

To prepare for the Jubilee and the anticipated arrival of as many as thirty million pilgrims during the year 2000, many of the city's streets and traffic patterns have undergone a radical reorganization—an occurrence that is bound to have an impact on future bus routes, still the principal form of public transportation. (In light of this situation, it is always advisable to call ahead to confirm both travel directions and visiting hours.)

Yet, while Rome is one of the most tantalizing cities in the world to visit, one which has drawn such poetic luminaries as Goethe, Keats, and Byron, not to mention the novelists Charles Dickens, Henry James, and Edith Wharton, it also remains one of the most multifaceted and complex of the world's capitals, and the same could be said for its museums. While one may easily be dazzled by the hidden riches inside the city's villas and palaces, trying to comprehend the complex iconography and history associated with them, as well as with the works of art within their walls, can present a somewhat daunting challenge.

Armed with only rusty Latin, and a dim memory of Greek and Roman mythology, I embarked on one of the great intellectual adventures of my writing career thus far, one that took me into the stacks at the Victoria & Albert Museum in London, the American Library and Bibliothèque Forney in Paris, and the research library at the American Academy in Rome. As I prepared my bibliography for this volume, I felt deeply moved by and grateful to the many fine authors who assisted me in my own pilgrimage of understanding, including E. H. Gombrich, Georgina Masson, H. V. Morton, Francis Haskell, and Giorgio Vasari. Yet, above all, I am profoundly indebted to the City of Rome itself, whose lengthy, complex, and turbulent history, has endowed me with an ever so much larger view of the world and its manifold possibilities.

With this volume (as with the three others that have preceded it on Paris, London, and Berlin), it is my fervent hope that readers and voyagers, even if they accompany me only in spirit, while comfortably settled in their favorite armchair, will journey with me to discover some of the world's lesser-known treasures in and around one of its best-known cities.

Each one of the museums I have come to know through writing this book has proven to be a storehouse of knowledge, as well as a repository of that which is best in all of us—our eternal quest for the authentic and novel, as well as the beautiful. Like the pilgrims and intrepid travelers who first came to the Eternal City, we now have the delightful opportunity to admire these exceptional collections— a timeless endeavor to extend hopefully into this new millennium.

Numerical Legend for Museum Sites In and Around Rome

(see Map on pages 14–15)

1 Art Center ACEA-Centrale
Montemartini
The ACEA Art Center at the
Montemartini Power Station

2 Aula Ottagona nelle Terme
di Diocleziano
The Octagonal Hall in the Baths
of Diocletian

3 Casino del Bel Respiro
The Bel Respiro Casino

4 Castello Ruspoli
The Ruspoli Castle

5 Galleria Corsini d'Arte Antica
a Palazzo Corsini
The National Gallery of Classical Art
in the Corsini Palace

6 Galleria Doria Pamphilj
The Doria Pamphilj Gallery

7 Mostra Permanente di Carrozze
The Permanent Exhibition of Carriages

8 Museo Archeologico Nazionale
di Palestrina
The National Archaeological Museum
of Palestrina

9 Museo Nazionale di Arte Orientale
The National Museum of Oriental Art

10 Museo Barracco
The Barracco Museum

11 Museo del Burcardo
The Burcardo Theater Museum

12 Museo della Casina delle Civette
The Museum of the Swiss Cottage
of the Owls

13 Museo della Ceramica-Palazzo Brugiotti
The Ceramic Museum in the
Brugiotti Palace

14 Museo Criminologico di Roma
The Rome Museum of Criminology

15 Museo Donazione Umberto Mastroianni
The Umberto Mastroianni Museum

16 Museo Ebraico di Roma
The Jewish Museum of Rome

17 Museo Giacomo Manzù-Ardea
The Giacomo Manzù Museum-Ardea

18 Museo Giorgio De Chirico
The Giorgio De Chirico Museum

19 Museo Mario Praz
The Mario Praz Museum

20 Palazzo Massimo alle Terme-Museo
Nazionale Romano
The National Roman Museum
in the Massimo Palace

21 Museo Napoleonico
The Napoleonic Museum

22 Museo delle Navi Romane
di Fiumicino
The Museum of Roman Ships
at Fiumicino

23 Museo Nazionale Etrusco
di Villa Giulia
The National Etruscan Museum
in the Villa Giulia

24 Museo dell'Olio della Sabina
The Sabine Olive Oil Museum

25 Museo dello Sbarco di Anzio
The Anzio Beachhead Museum

26 Palazzo Altemps-Museo
Nazionale Roma
The National Roman Museum
in the Palazzo Altemps

27 Palazzo Farnese a Caprarola
The Farnese Palace at Caprarola

28 Palazzo I Galleria Spada
The Spada Palace and Gallery

29 Villa Farnesina
The Villa Farnesina

30 Villa Madama
The Villa Madama

Map of Museum Sites In and Around Rome

(see Numerical Legend on page 13)

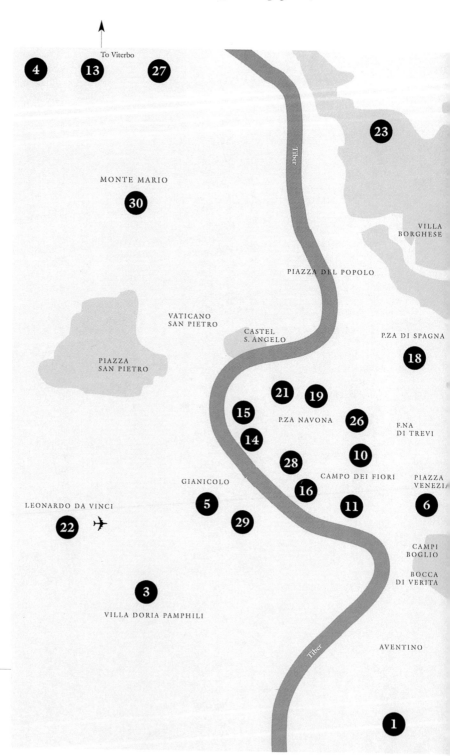

CATACOMBE DI PRISCILLA

VIA VENETO

PORTA PIA

TERMINI

TRAIN STATION

To Palestrina

FORI IMPERIALE

To Ardea

COLOSSEO

S. GIOVANNI
IN LATERANO

APPIA ANTICA

E.U.R.

To Anzio

To Rieti

THE COLOSSAL STATUE OF ATHENA
IS A COPY OF A BRONZE WORK
FROM THE END OF THE FIFTH CENTURY B.C.
IT IS ONE OF THE FINEST KNOWN
COPIES OF THE *VELLETRI ATHENA*
(NOW IN THE LOUVRE).
THE DIESEL-RUN TOSI ENGINE WAS
INSTALLED IN 1932.

Art Center ACEA-Centrale Montemartini

The ACEA Art Center
at the Montemartini Power Station

Via Ostiense, N. 106
Rome 00154
Tel: 06/574–8042

Open Tuesday through Friday,
10:00 A.M. to 6:00 P.M.
Open Saturday and Sunday
10:00 A.M. to 7:00 P.M.
Open Monday only for
pre-booked tours.

Metro: Garbatella

Cafeteria on premises.

Y O U can almost hear the roar of
the turbines. You marvel at the height
of the immense diesel-powered
generators, as grandiose as some of
Rome's monuments. It's hard to miss
the quadrants once used to measure
pressure, temperature, and electrical
power. In the middle of this Italian
Art Nouveau edifice there are gigantic
steam boilers, reminiscent of ships
in dry dock. Inside a vast and
overwhelming engine-room stand a
row of Roman marble gods, draped
in togas, eternal in their pride and
dignity. Are we in the midst of a
surrealistic masterpiece, worthy of a
Giorgio De Chirico? Or are we seeing
a unique blend of ancient art and
industrial archaeology? Perhaps the
answer is: something of both.

Inspired by the Musée d'Orsay in
Paris, the first major institution to
transform industrial architecture into
an art museum (in this instance a
train station), the management
at the Capitoline Museums and the
Municipal Superintendance of
Cultural Assets saw the possibility of
transforming Rome's former power
plant complex into a spacious and
dramatically different exhibition hall
for over 400 pieces of sculpture
originally displayed in the Capitoline
Museum. It has proved to be an
aesthetic solution evoking both awe
and appreciation. Suddenly, these
statues no longer seem cold and
daunting figures, but instead take on
a whole new poignancy and imme-
diacy in light of their proximity to the
brute force of technology.

Located along the Via Ostiense
between the General Market and the

THE FAÇADE OF THE ACEA ART CENTER
IS A RARE EXAMPLE OF
INDUSTRIAL ARCHAEOLOGICAL
RECOVERY IN ROME.
NOTE THE ELEGANT "CAMBELLOTTI"
STREET LAMP, NAMED AFTER
ITS DESIGNER DUILIO CAMBELLOTTI,
WHO ALSO CREATED
SOME OF THE STAINED-GLASS WINDOWS
FOR THE SWISS COTTAGE
OF THE OWLS.

AMONG THE STATUES IN THE FORMER FURNACE ROOM
ARE A NEO-ATTIC RHYTON-SHAPED FOUNTAIN
(HALF HORN, HALF ANIMAL) FROM THE FIRST CENTURY A.D.,
AND A COLOSSAL DEMETER,
A ROMAN COPY OF A MID-FIFTH-CENTURY A.D. WORK FROM GREECE.
BOTH WORKS ORIGINALLY ORNAMENTED
THE GARDENS OF THE ROMAN ARTS PATRON, GAIUS MAECENAS.

left bank of the Tiber, the Montemartini Power Station was inaugurated in June 1912 by the Municipal Electricity Company AEM (currently known as ACEA). Measuring 20,000 square feet, it was the first publicly owned power plant to generate electricity in Rome.

Together with the Castel Madama hydroelectric power station built a few years later, it was constructed to provide light for over half the streets and squares in the city, with a lighting intensity double that of the previous norm. Although it began with only 1,152 users in 1912, by 1915 that figure had risen to 21,093, and twice that amount by 1920. During the same time span, private consumption jumped from 56,000 kilowatts to almost eleven million kilowatts.

When the Allies entered Rome in June 1944, the Montemartini Power Station was the only power plant still generating electricity. Thanks to the company's strategy of flying the Holy See's white and yellow flags, the Germans had been deceived into thinking that the power plant belonged to the Vatican State, and thus had spared Montemartini from otherwise certain destruction.

It was technological obsolescence that ultimately determined the plant's demise. For the past thirty years the ancient diesel and coal-fed Franco Tosi furnaces and turbines have been silent, replaced by gas-fed power plants which are both cleaner and more efficient. Thanks to meticulous restoration work in 1989 and 1990, Rome's first electricity plant was initially transformed into a multi-media conference center, used for temporary exhibitions and conclaves. An admirable effort surely, but nothing too remarkable. Montemartini's true renaissance began two years ago, with the restoration of the Capitoline museums and the planning for the Jubilee Year. Would all the sculptures have to be stored in warehouses? It soon became apparent that Montemartini's vast cathedral-like space could offer an ideal home for some of the Eternal City's finest statuary and artifacts. The result has proved to be so pleasing and accept-able to the public, that what was once viewed as a temporary alternative exhibition space has now evolved into a unique, permanent institution which simultaneously pays tribute to the triumphs of Roman archaeology and the Industrial Revolution.

With the unification of Italy in 1870, Rome was declared the capital of the country. As the new monarchy of Victor Emmanuel II embarked on an ambitious rebuilding program of the ancient city, between 1870 and 1885 the archaeologist Rodolfo Lanciani was tallying the greatest number of finds since the late six-teenth century: 705 amphorae, 2,360 lamps, 1,824 inscriptions, 77 columns of pink marble, 313 pieces of columns, 157 capitals, 18 sarcophagi, 36,679 gold, silver, and bronze coins.

Excavations carried out in 1870 near the Esquiline, Quirinal, and Viminal Hills, reaped a rich artistic harvest from the *horti*, palatial Roman villas surrounded by verdant gardens filled with splendid marble statuary, that were built by aristocratic families during the late Republican Age, and which later became the property of the Emperor and his entourage. Frescoes, mosaics, sculptures—even an entire necropolis—came to light after having been buried for centuries.

Montemartini's monumental Furnace Room, with its blackened furnaces and extensive ramps, imparts an entirely new aura to statues which were unearthed on these ancient Roman estates. Excavations in the gardens of Gaius Cilnius Maecenas (70–8 B.C.), the Roman statesman and advisor to Augustus, have yielded a poignant reminder of the ancients' veneration for the arts: white marble statues which have been identified as Muses, including an exquisitely draped statue representing Melpomene (the Greek Muse of Tragedy), together with a series of portrait herms of literary figures, a reminder that Maecenas was a friend and patron of Horace and Virgil. Even more noteworthy is the *Head of an Amazon*, an exceptional marble copy of a bronze work that was entered in a competition held at Ephesus between 444 and 430 B.C. (The statue is believed to be a copy of a bronze by Polycletus, who won the contest, beating out such artistic rivals as Kresilas and Phidias.)

The *Horti Tauriani* formed perhaps the biggest estate in the Esquiline area, stretching over eighty acres, according to ancient literary sources. The splendid villa and property owned by Statilius Taurus so aroused the jealousy and greed of Agrippina, the wife of the Emperor Claudius, that she incited Tarquitium Priscus to accuse the senator of embezzling and practicing magic. Taurus did not wait for the verdict to be announced, preferring to commit suicide. Subsequently, all his possessions were confiscated by the Emperor.

Among the artworks that Agrippina coveted was a splendid statue of *Igea* wrapped in an elabo-rately draped toga, tunic, and stole, and wearing an arm bracelet studded with gems, identified as a late

Republican reproduction of a fourth century B.C. statue. Yet perhaps the finest masterpieces from this garden are the two giant marble kraters, one decorated with a frieze illustrating a lively Dionysian celebration of drinking and dancing, the other depicting the wedding of Paris with Helen of Troy, in a style inspired by Archaic and Classical art.

A lengthy gallery of statues from the late Republican era in the Engine Room leads the way to one of the museùms's greatest examples of classical Greek sculpture, a reconstruction of the *tympanum* (pediment) from the Temple of Apollo the Healer (now known as the *Temple of Apollo Sosianus*). Originally built in 431 B.C., it was commissioned to fulfill a vow made after a terrible plague that had decimated the population of Rome. Rebuilt several times since then, the last rendition of the temple was undertaken by Gaius Sosius, who conquered the Jews in 34 B.C. and became consul in 32 B.C. A political ally of Mark Anthony, he was sentenced to death after Anthony's defeat at Actium in 31 B.C., but was

THESE HELLENISTIC STATUES WERE DISCOVERED ON THE ESQUILINE HILL
IN THE GARDEN OF MAECENAS,
AND DATE FROM THE FIRST AND SECOND CENTURIES A.D.
THE LARGE MARBLE KRATERS ARE FROM THE FIRST CENTURY A.D.
THE INTEGRATION OF STATUES, KRATERS, AND FOUNTAINS
WAS PART OF A SCHEME TO DOMESTICATE NATURE AND CREATE
AN ARTIFICIAL SETTING.

A PANORAMIC VIEW OF THE FORMER MACHINE ROOM;
THE HELMETED STATUE OF ATHENA AGAINST THE FAR BACK WALL
WAS ONCE PART OF A LONG PORTICO WHICH FLANKED THE VIA LATA,
NOW THE VIA DEL CORSO, NEAR THE PIAZZA SCIARRA.

later pardoned and readmitted to the political circle of Octavian. (With the discovery in 1937 of the temple's podium, and its identification as having been constructed under the supervision of Sosius, the find was renamed the *Temple of Apollo Sosianus.*)

The reassembled *tympanum* of nine sculptures is breathtaking, and is rightly regarded by archaeologists as one of the most important groups of Greek sculptures from the fifth century B.C. in Rome. After patient research and restoration, scholars have been able to establish that the pediment's fragmented statuary illustrates Hercules' ninth labor. Under the orders of King Eurystheus, Hercules, in the company of Theseus, embarked on an expedition against the Amazons, with the ultimate aim of capturing the belt of the Amazons' Queen

Hippolyta. Yet even as we marvel at the Greeks' mastery over marble and the human form, we can only imagine the spectacular effect of the original pediment, when the sculptures were painted and decorated with gilded bronze weapons, clothing, and hair.

Curator Marina Bertolotti has considered the impression this site and novel exhibition produces: "At times, the machines appear to loom in their massiveness and the crowd of gods seems to be present at their triumph," she writes. "At other times, the machines seem to be just a backdrop of discarded carcasses, and the gods celebrate their victory over them." While visitors may find this museum a visual challenge, few will dispute the claim that this unique exhibition at the former Montemartini Power Plant is a triumph of the imagination.

Aula Ottagona nelle Terme di Diocleziano

The Octagonal Hall in the Baths of Diocletian

Via Giuseppe Romita, N. 8
Rome 00186
Tel: 06/487–0690

**Open Tuesday through Saturday,
9:00 A.M. to 5:00 P.M.
Open Sunday and holidays
9:00 A.M. to 2:00 P.M.**

**Bus: 64, 137, 492, 910
Metro A: Repubblica**

THE PRESENT-DAY ENTRANCE
TO THE OCTAGONAL HALL
IN THE BATHS OF DIOCLETIAN
IS UNDERNEATH
ONE OF THE ENORMOUS ARCHED
WINDOWS THAT ONCE
PROVIDED THE ROOM WITH LIGHT.
THE HALL'S PLAN IS RECTANGULAR
ON THE OUTSIDE
AND OCTAGONAL ON THE INSIDE.

T H E Baths of Diocletian, begun by the Emperor Maximian in A.D. 298 and completed by his co-Emperor Diocletian around A.D. 305, once formed the largest bath complex in ancient Rome. (Olympiodorus of Thebes suggests that they were used simultaneously by as many as 3,000 bathers, which is almost double the capacity of the Baths of Caracalla.) For the Romans, the baths were not just a place to wash, take a swim, enjoy exercise, or gossip; they also housed magnificent art collections.

Knowing this, it seems altogether fitting that the Octagonal Hall (on the southwest corner of the central block containing the Baths of Diocletian), has been transformed into a stunning gallery for sculptures in bronze and marble from the great Imperial Baths of Rome, including the Baths of Trajan, Caracalla, Constantine, and Diocletian, in use from the second to the fourth centuries A.D.

The great Imperial *thermae* in Rome were laid out as rectangular venues incorporating libraries, lecture halls, and conversation areas, which were surrounded by extensive gardens. A central block of buildings contained the baths themselves, along with dressing rooms and gymnasiums (*palaestrae*).

Built with concrete that was poured into ingeniously engineered brick shells, these edifices were reinforced at stress points with two-foot-square bricks (*bipedali*).The baths were heated by means of a *hypocaust,* a system that allowed hot air to circulate under a floor that was suspended on piles of bricks, as well as around the walls through hollow terra-cotta tubes *(tubuli)*.

The Octagonal Hall is rectangular on the outside, octagonal on the inside, with four large, semicircular niches. It is capped with an umbrella-shaped dome composed of eight segments which meet at the top in a ring, leaving an eight-sided opening which is glassed in. The present pavement does not correspond with the ancient one, which is at a lower level and is now on view in the building's basement.

The vast room originally had two enormous windows with semicircular arched heads facing south and west; one is the gallery's current entrance, the other has been blocked off. A series of doors linked the Hall with the gardens, which surrounded the central complex of baths, as well as with the gymnasium and the rooms leading to the hot bath *(caldarium)*. The walls, which were built with brick-faced concrete, were once covered with marble and stucco, none of which remains today. The absence of a heating system, the ample light, and the connecting doors to other parts of the complex, suggest this room was used as a passageway. However, a sixteenth-century account mentions that the room contained a pool, indicating that the Hall might at some point have been used as a small *frigidarium* (cold bath) for washing.

After Vitigis, King of the Goths, cut off Rome's aqueducts in A.D. 537, the area was abandoned, its inhabitants moving down into the lower part of the city near the Tiber. Between 1561 and 1563, Pope Pius IV had the central hall of the Baths transformed into the Church of S. Maria degli Angeli (Saint Mary of the Angels), entrusting the project to Michelangelo. By the beginning of the seventeenth century, other rooms were being used as granaries, includ-

THE OCTAGONAL HALL STILL HAS ITS ORIGINAL BRICK VAULT, AN EIGHT-LOBED UMBRELLA DOME WITH AN OCTAGONAL SKYLIGHT. IT PROVIDES A MONUMENTAL SETTING FOR THESE EXCEPTIONAL BRONZE AND MARBLE STATUES, MANY OF WHICH WERE ONCE USED TO DECORATE ROMAN BATHS.

ing the Octagonal Hall. In the nineteenth century, the granaries were transformed by the Church into charitable institutions.

However, during Rome's reorganization at the end of the nineteenth century, this building took on a life of its own, first, as a school of gymnastics, then as a motion-picture theater, and finally, in 1928, becoming the Planetarium. An elegant canopy, formed by a geometric grid supported on slender metal columns with cast-iron capitals belonging to this latest phase, was retained for the gallery. (Only in 1987 was it possible to transform this hall into an exhibition area.)

Seeing the Octagonal Hall's strikingly unadorned space makes it

hard to conjure up the luxury that once characterized these ancient baths. Elaborately decorated with columns and capitals, stuccos, friezes, mosaics, and paintings, the bath complex also contained a dazzling assembly of statues in bronze and in marble painted in vivid colors. Although it is difficult to confirm the original placement of the statues in the various parts of the bath complexes, it is now known that the statues were set in niches and fixed in place with metal rods, traces of which remain on several sculptures or on their bases.

Sculptures were not only used as decoration in the baths, but also were displayed for public enjoyment and even to promote the Roman Empire's ideology. The most prevalent subjects were gods, athletes, and portraits of famous individuals. Most of the works in the Octagonal Hall are copies or variations on masterpieces of Classical Greek art, made either before the construction of the building or specifically for the baths in which they were found.

Two authentic bronze masterpieces from the Hellenistic era take their rightful place in the center of the gallery: *The Prince of the Baths* and *The Boxer of the Baths*. Cast with the lost-wax process, these two famous bronzes were found together in 1885 in the Convent of San Silvestro on the slopes of the Quirinal—they apparently were used to decorate the Baths of Constantine built around A.D. 315 on the Quirinal.

The larger-than-life-size statue of the Prince is portrayed in "heroic nudity," and exudes a regal and stately aura. His head, rather small in proportion compared to the rest of the body, is notable for its impressive realism. His high cheekbones, aquiline nose, pointed and dimpled chin, and spotty whiskers all suggest an intended portrait. Dating from the middle of the second century B.C., scholars are inclined to identify the portrait as being that of a Hellenistic ruler or a Roman general.

Next to this awe-inspiring youth sits the exhausted figure of a middle-aged boxer overcome with fatigue after a match. He is nude, although his hands and forearms are protected by long lace-up leather boxing gloves with thumb articulations and lined fur cuffs. What is immediately striking is the artist's acute sense of observation and the almost brutal realism with which he renders the fighter's wounds—a far cry from the classical idealization of the athlete. Scars and bruises are visible all over his body, especially on his face: there are cuts on his cheek and forehead, a broken and deformed nose, a cut lip, a swollen right eye and ears. Red copper inlay indicates the boxer's fresh facial wounds and the blood dripping from his face onto his right arm and thigh. Since the statue's original glass eyes are lost, we can only imagine the pain they must have conveyed. Although the work was once attributed to Apollonius son of Nestor, the Athenian sculptor who signed the famous Belvedere torso in the Vatican, current scholarship identifies the statue as being a late fourth-century B.C. figure from the entourage of Lysippus, or a late-Hellenistic production.

THE LARGER-THAN-LIFE-SIZE
PRINCE OF THE BATHS IS SHOWN
IN "HEROIC NUDITY"—
HIS STANCE IS BOTH REGAL
AND SOLEMN.

The Hall's other statues are arranged along the walls; made of polished white marble, their idealized forms contrast sharply with the two bronze figures in the center of the gallery. Ten of them come from the Baths of Caracalla, built between A.D. 212 and A.D. 216. The *Herms of Apollo* and *Mercury,* notable for their elaborate curly hairstyles, were sculpted in the second century A.D.

As protectors of athletic contests, such herms were usually found in gymnasiums, libraries, and gardens.

Given the plundering and vandalism to which the Baths of Diocletian were subjected for centuries, it is all the more remarkable to see some of the sculptures that once ornamented this ancient complex. The most outstanding of these is the *Aphrodite of Cnidus,* a larger than life-size copy dating from early Imperial Rome, inspired by Praxiteles' celebrated Greek original. She was uncovered with her companion, a larger-than-life-size copy of a fifth-century B.C. male torso, also from the same period.

As impressive as these two statues are, both pale beside the *Venus of Cyrene,* shown in all her glory and beauty, just after she has risen from the foaming waves that had given birth to her. Her missing arms seem to be raised to wring the water out of her wet hair; her tunic, carelessly tossed over a dolphin with a fish in its mouth, reminds us that she has only just emerged from the sea. This Venus was discovered in the Bath of Cyrene after a storm in 1913, apparently quite by accident, while two army officers were taking a walk. One of them carried a stick and struck something hard in the sand as he paced along. So curious was his companion that he returned later to the very spot the officer had hit, and in this way, the statue was found.

Thanks to the handsome restoration of the Octagonal Hall, we can better appreciate the magnificence of Rome's ancient baths, while contemplating a stunning collection of sculpture—which we owe in large measure to the serendipity as well as the science of archaeology.

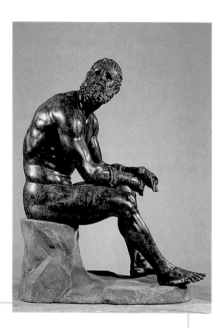

THIS ATHLETE,
CALLED *THE BOXER OF THE BATHS*
IS PORTRAYED
AS A SURVIVOR OF MANY CONTESTS.
NO LONGER YOUNG,
THE WEARY WEIGHT OF HIS BODY
SPEAKS ELOQUENTLY
OF ALL THAT HE HAS ENDURED.

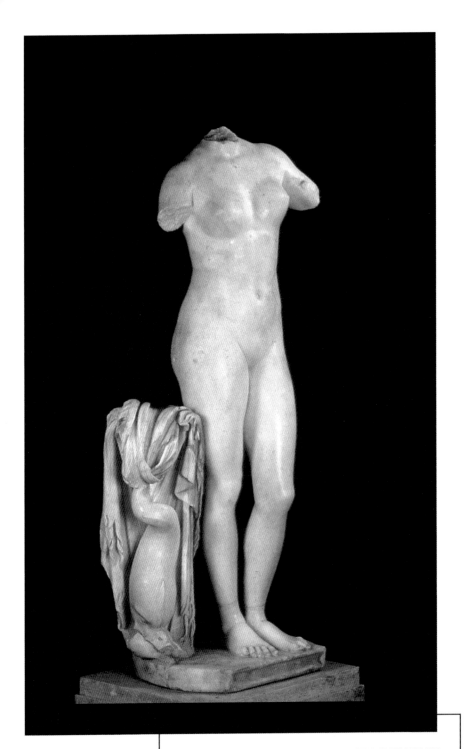

THIS HEADLESS *VENUS OF CYRENE,* EMERGING FROM THE SEA
IS BASED ON A FAMOUS (NOW LOST) PAINTING BY APELLES,
WHICH DEPICTS THE GODDESS
AS HAVING JUST EMERGED FROM THE WAVES,
AND WRINGING WATER FROM HER HAIR.

THE SOUTHERN FACADE OF THE CASINO DEL BEL RESPIRO
OVERLOOKS THE SECRET GARDEN.
IN THE CENTER OF THE GARDEN IS A BRONZE COPY OF
PIETRO TACCA'S SEVENTEENTH-CENTURY
FOUNTAIN IN THE PIAZZA DELL' ANNUNZIATA IN FLORENCE.
IT REPLACED ALGARDI'S STUCCO *FOUNTAIN*
OF THE MARINE TIGERS.

Casino del Bel Respiro

The Bel Respiro Casino

Via Aurelia Antica, N.111
Rome 00153

**Visits only by pre-arranged
guided tours with
Associazione Citta Nascosta.**
Tel: 06/331–6059

Bus: 31, 44, 791, 982

S ITUATED by the western walls of
Rome near the San Pancrazio Gate,
the Villa Pamphilj is the largest public
park in Rome, a haven for joggers
and cyclists, as well as picnickers.
Because of its vast size (close to four
hundred acres), few people know
that it contains the last example of
Renaissance-inspired Neoclassical
architecture in Rome, the enchanting
Casino del Bel Respiro. Created
between 1644 and 1648 by the
sculptor Alessandro Algardi (1598–
1654) and the painter Giovan
Francesco Grimaldi (1606–1680), the
Casino was conceived as a *palazzetto*
for Cardinal Camillo Pamphilj, the
nephew of Pope Innocent X.

The site of special celebrations
until the nineteenth century, the
edifice acquired its present name
because of the hillside estate's bracing
air. (Today, after significant restoration, it is used by the Presidency
of the Council of Ministers and the
Italian government, when it is not
being shown through pre-arranged
tours.)

Since neither Algardi nor Grimaldi
had any experience or background
in architecture, it may seem surprising
that they were chosen for this
commission. Although Gian Lorenzo
Bernini was regarded then as the
greatest Baroque sculptor and architect (he would eventually be invited
to Paris to work on the Louvre and
sculpt portraits of Louis XIV), he was
not commissioned to design the
Casino. It seems that this was not a
propitious period for Bernini; while
he was still working on the left
bell-tower of Saint Peter's, serious
cracks had appeared in the underlying

structure and in 1646, all of his work had to be demolished. Nor did it help that he had been associated with Innocent X's predecessor, the much-reviled Urban VIII. (This latter pope's petty war against the Farnese, coupled with his extravagance and waste, caused the heavily taxed Roman populace to break out into riotous jubilation at the news of his death.)

All of this proved opportune for Bernini's greatest rival, Francesco Borromini (1599–1667), who proposed a singular project for Cardinal Pamphilj's villa, that was a cross between a fortress with bastions at the four corners and a *palazzina* complete with statues and sculptures; inside, the rooms were to lead off from a central octagonal drawing-room with niches and columns. The project also involved the celebration of the new papacy: Borromini's plans were calculated in such a way that the sun's rays would strike the foot of a statue of Innocent X once a year, on the same day and at the same hour wherein he had been elected pope!

However, the pope's nephew was obviously unimpressed, since the project never got beyond the blueprint stage. Instead, Cardinal Pamphilj retained Algardi, whom he had met when the latter was appointed curator and restorer of the celebrated Ludovisi collection of ancient sculptures. This artist chose to model the Casino's design on his studies of the Renaissance architect Palladio, as well as of Hadrian's Villa. This is confirmed by an account from the seventeenth-century art connoisseur Filippo Baldinucci: "Algardi received from Don Camillo Pamphilj the undertaking to construct the handsome Villa del Bel Respiro at San Pancrazio, with extremely fine ornaments such as fountains and the like, and using a project by Palladio;

he revealed himself to a marvelous degree dextrous in the stucco-work on the lower floor, having gone for this particular purpose to Tivoli, to make drawings of various objects from Hadrian's Villa."

Algardi's Casino is perhaps the last example of that Renaissance taste which was consolidated during the Mannerist period, and which continued to be popular during the first half of the seventeenth century, when façades were covered with bas-reliefs and statues. There is little doubt that Algardi was inspired by two other great seventeenth-century Roman palaces, the Villa Borghese, commissioned by Cardinal Scipione, the nephew of Paul V, and the Villa Ludovisi, contracted by the Bolognese Ludovico Ludovisi, the nephew of Gregory XV (which was destroyed in the nineteenth century to construct a district of the same name).

The elegant exterior ornamentation and statuary are beautifully integrated into the northern façade, thanks to two orders of five bays each, a feature that was inspired by the now lost Villa del Pigneto designed by Pietro da Cortona. (Still, Algardi's lack of experience as an architect is apparent in the odd height of the façade's central atrium arch, which hinders the central windows' alignment with the other windows on either side of it.)

Some of the sculptures disposed along the Casino's exterior are Hellenistic—such as the sarcophagi bas-reliefs at the foot of the first order and on the attic—while others are from the seventeenth century, such as the arms and trophies on either side of the atrium and the cameos of emperors' heads. Often, they are a blend of both periods, having been reconstituted out of badly damaged classical originals.

THE FIRST-FLOOR ROTUNDA FEATURES PAINTINGS OF FANCIFUL LANDSCAPES ATTRIBUTED
TO GIOVANNI FRANCESCO GRIMALDI AND FRANCESCO PENTIMELI.
THE ROOM'S STATUES MAY BE CONSIDERED MORE SEVENTEENTH CENTURY
THAN CLASSICAL, SINCE ARTISTS FROM THE PERIOD
THOUGHT NOTHING OF TRANSFORMING A BADLY MUTILATED TORSO
INTO A FINISHED STATUE.

The *piano nobile* (first floor) is roughly square in plan, enhanced by a central rotunda, and double the height of the surrounding rooms. Light comes exclusively from the top of the cupola and the sloping windows placed at the level of the roof-terrace. Inside the ground-floor rotunda, between the large doors opening onto the adjacent rooms, there are niches that hold ancient statues (which were heavily restored in the seventeenth century). Above the doors, beveled gray marble frames surround paintings of imaginary landscapes attributed to Giovanni

THE ROTUNDA IS
THE MOST RICHLY DECORATED ROOM IN THE CASINO.
THE MEDALLIONS IN THE VAULTING
ILLUSTRATE FIGURES FROM THE ROMAN EMPIRE,
INCLUDING THE SHE-WOLF,
THE GODDESS OF VICTORY, AND THE GODDESS OF ROME.
THIS ROOM EXEMPLIFIES
BOTH ALGARDI'S AND HIS PATRON'S PASSION
FOR CLASSICAL ANTIQUITY.

THE CENTRAL TONDO IN THE ROTUNDA
CONTAINS A VERY FINE STUCCO BAS-RELIEF OF THE PAMPHILJ
COAT-OF-ARMS SUPPORTED BY TWO PUTTI.

Francesco Grimaldi and Franceso Pentimeli.

As was true of most wealthy and cultivated art patrons of his era, Camillo Pamphilj was eager to have a residence built for him that would show he was conversant with the myths and legends of the Hellenistic world. Thus, the rotunda's niches are filled with statues of Aphrodite, a Roman warrior with a head of a Gaul (originally a Roman copy of Polycletus's *Spearman*), a Roman copy of a Greek athlete, and a statue of Athena (formerly an Amazon). Another reminder of the ancient world is at one's feet: in the center of the fine terra-cotta floor is a *tondo* with small tiles in a herringbone pattern from the Roman period, perhaps unearthed from the villa area itself.

Most of the rooms on this floor were heavily restored during this century, with the exception of the *trompe l'oeil* ceiling in the southeast room, (now a dining room), which is elaborately decorated with a central eighteenth-century tondo depicting *Flora*, the goddess of spring. At the corners of the ceiling, four elaborate supports are drawn with volutes, as if they were holding up the central tondo; each support has a couple of *putti* (cherubs) reclining on the volutes, a monochrome oval blue cameo illustrating a season, and the heraldic lily of the Pamphili.

Downstairs, the ground floor is an inverted version of the floor above, the south room acting as a vestibule with access to a dazzling Secret Garden. All four areas on the ground floor retain Algardi's original, pastel-colored stucco decorations on the vaults, whose symbolism and iconography are extremely complex. They were meant to celebrate Cardinal

THE HERCULES ROOM,
WHOSE STUCCOS WERE DESIGNED BY ALGARDI,
AND WHOSE WALL FRESCOES WERE EXECUTED
BY GRIMALDI,
ILLUSTRATES THE TWELVE LABORS
AND OTHER EPISODES
IN THE LIFE OF
THE MYTHOLOGICAL HERO, HERCULES,
WHO PERSONIFIED PHYSICAL STRENGTH
AS WELL AS THE COURAGE
TO TRIUMPH OVER EVIL AND ATTAIN IMMORTALITY.
HERCULES COULD ALSO BE
CONSIDERED AN EXAMPLE OF MORAL STRENGTH
THAT WAS IN HARMONY WITH
CHRISTIAN DOCTRINE.

Camillo, and through him his uncle the pope, and to represent the antiquarian interests of the artist and his cultural circle as representatives of seventeenth-century Classicism.

In the "Room of Roman Costumes," named after the decorative themes in the vault, Algardi designed three large panels depicting *Apollo, Minerva,* and *Justice,* all allusions to his patron's studies of poetry, literature, and law. (As flattering as these allusions might have been, Innocent X was so unimpressed with his nephew's capacities that he appointed someone else to the post of secretary-of-state.)

The room also attests to the archaeological interests of Algardi and his circle: some scenes were drawn from ancient Roman bas-reliefs, such as those of the life of Trajan from the Arch of Constantine, whereas the allegories of Victory, Peace, and Justice in the tondo at the edges of the vaulting were copies of Imperial Roman medals.

While the stuccowork in this room is impressive enough, the most splendidly decorated room in the Casino is, without a doubt, the Rotunda. On the walls, pairs of Ionic pilaster strips alternate with niches, each of which contains statues or doors to adjacent rooms. Starting from the door in a clockwise direction, stucco panels illustrate the four cardinal virtues: Strength, Prudence, Temperance, and Justice, followed by Generosity and the three Christian virtues of Faith, Hope, and Charity.

Most dazzling of all is the ceiling, richly decorated with delicate stuccowork, segmented by *fasciae,* which are a continuation of the wall's pilaster strips. To add variety, the first concentric circle of the vault alternates heraldic olive branches and floral garlands. The larger areas between the vault's fasciae are deco-

rated with medallions of figures from the Roman Empire, including the goddess of Victory, the She-Wolf, and the goddess of Rome, positioned prominently in the lunette above the doorway to the vestibule.

Still, when it comes to complex decorative iconography, it would be difficult to surpass the Hercules Room, where the Grimaldi frescoes illustrate the Twelve Labors of Hercules, the son of Jupiter, who was deified for his trials and labors on earth. In one panel, *Hercules Helping Atlas Sustain the Globe* (a direct allusion to Camillo's role in helping to sustain the papacy), the globe bears the zodiac signs of Leo and Virgo, under which the conclave that led to the pope's election was held, as well as the sign of Scorpio, under which Camillo was made cardinal.

After visiting this magnificent *palazzetto* with its wondrous stuccowork and intriguing iconography, one can well understand why Rome was considered the apex of the artistic world in the seventeenth century. The combined virtuosity and talent in the Casino del Bel Respiro provides a striking example of Italian artistry that has been lovingly preserved for all to appreciate and admire.

Castello Ruspoli

The Ruspoli Castle

Vignanello, Viterbo 01039
Tel: 0761/755–338

Open Sunday
10:00 A.M. to 1:00 P.M.
April 1 through October 30.
Visits only by pre-arranged
guided tours.

By train: Leaves from the train
station Piazzale Flaminio,
near Piazza del Popolo. (It is a
two-hour trip to Vignanello.)
By car: Take the Via Cassia (S2)
north to Vignanello, Viterbo.

THIS PANORAMIC VIEW OF THE
RUSPOLI CASTLE INCLUDES A CORNER
OF ITS SPLENDID SIXTEENTH-CENTURY
ITALIANATE GARDEN.
THE GARDEN'S CENTRAL PARTERRES
FEATURE THE INITIALS OF THE
PRINCESS OTTAVIA
AND THOSE OF HER CHILDREN.

NINETY minutes north of the
bustling city of Rome, high in the
hills of Vignanello in the Alto Lazio
region (famed for its olive oil and
hazelnuts), is the ancestral castle
of the Ruspoli family. With its dark,
thick stone façade, plunging dry
moat, and crenelated walls, this
Medieval edifice towers imposingly
over the town's church and red-tiled
rooftops and the surrounding verdant
landscape. Originally constructed
as a Benedictine monastery in 853,
and rebuilt as a fortress around 1200,
it has been in the hands of the
Ruspoli family since 1500, resistant
to invasion, pillage, or destruction.

To enter the castle one still has to
cross a drawbridge suspended on
thick iron chains, and while one may
be inclined to announce oneself
via one of the palace's heavy iron
knockers, it would be advisable to use
the electronic intercom system
instead. Greeting visitors at the door
is none other than the castle's
châtelaine, Principessa Claudia
Ruspoli, who for a small fee provides
visitors with the opportunity to
walk in the footsteps of her illustrious
and sometimes infamous ancestors.

"To appreciate the castle's
architecture and garden, it is important to know something about our
family history," says Ruspoli, pointing
to an elaborate family tree painted on
one of the whitewashed walls in the
monumental front entrance. Tracing
her family back 1200 years, she notes
that her ancestors first came to Rome
with the legions of Charlemagne.
"Known as Mario Lo Scotto (Mario
the Scotsman), the name was soon
changed to Marescotti. He settled in

OVER THE FIREPLACE IS THE COAT-OF-ARMS IN GILDED WOOD
THAT COMES FROM THE PALAZZO ORSINI AT BOMARZO.

Bologna, where he founded a family that was to become very wealthy and powerful over the next 600 years."

So powerful, in fact, that by 1531 Alessandro Farnese (who became Pope Paul III in 1534), felt it was only fitting to present the castle and fiefdom of Vignanello as a wedding gift to his niece Ortensia Farnese, when she married a courtier at the papal court named Ercole Sforza Marescotti. The couple commissioned Renaissance architect Antonio da Sangallo the Younger to transform the rude fortress into a more comfortable villa. However, the marriage soon soured, and one night, in a fit of pique, Ortensia killed her husband

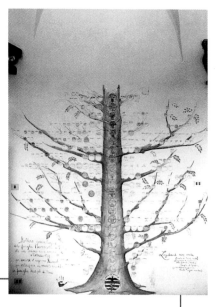

THE EXTENSIVE RUSPOLI FAMILY TREE,
WHICH EXTENDS
OVER TWELVE CENTURIES,
IS PAINTED ON THE PLASTER WALL.

with a fire poker.

Thanks to her familial connection to Pope Paul III, she spent only a few months imprisoned in the Castel Sant' Angelo, and was soon able to return to Vignanello. "One of the first things she did was to erase her husband's coat-of-arms wherever it appeared in the house," notes Ruspoli, pointing to a fireplace where only the Farnese fleur-de-lis remains. (Nonetheless, Ortensia did not undertake to destroy the severe portraits of illustrious Marescottis that dominate the dining room on the castle's second floor. To this day, no one in the Ruspoli family knows who painted them.)

By the end of the seventeenth century, through an arranged marriage that brought both money and respectability to the family, the Marescotti name was abandoned. "We adopted the Ruspoli name after the marriage of Sforza Marescotti to the wealthy Vittoria Ruspoli," explains Ruspoli.

The castle's frescoed ceilings and grisaille friezes were created in the eighteenth century, when the family's most illustrious member, Francesco Maria Ruspoli, took up residence. After consenting to finance a papal legion of 17,000 soldiers, Ruspoli was made a prince by Pope Clement XI, an event that was commemorated in a painting that still hangs in the Ruspoli palace in Rome (which is reproduced in an engraving on display in the castle at Vignanello). An active patron of the arts, he often invited his friend Handel to Vignanello to perform and compose at his leisure. It was here in 1707 that Handel wrote parts of *The Resurrection*, which he dedicated to his Roman patron.

While most of the castle's precious paintings and furniture were sold during this century in order to maintain the castle and liquidate the family's sizable debts, its greatest treasure remains intact and is well worth the visit: a very rare, early seventeenth-century parterre considered to be the finest of its kind in Italy. Conceived when the notorious Ortensia's nephew Marcantonio Marescotti married Ottavia Orsini, its geometrical design closely resembles those in Sebastiano Serlio's architectural treatise. According to family tradition, it was Ottavia Orsini (whose father had designed the famed gardens at Bomarzo), who laid out the fragrant parterre, which originally was made of sage and rosemary.

Yet, before Ottavia could even think of planting her garden, she first had to find a place to locate it. Undeterred by the fortress's placement atop a rocky crag, she saw to it

that part of the surrounding moat was filled in with tons of earth carried in by oxcart, and subsequently surrounded by stone ramparts. A bridge was then erected across the moat, linking the castle to the garden site.

Of rectangular shape, the garden is divided by four paths and subdivided into twelve compact parterres, all of an exacting geometry. In the center is a large oval fountain with four stone balusters. Ottavia's imprint upon the garden is underscored by the parterres' design, with the central bed nearest the castle featuring her initials, "O.O.," arranged in a cipher to encircle those of her two sons, Sforza and Galeazzo. (The significance of this motif is that it makes it possible to date the parterres with much greater exactitude than is usually the

THE UPSTAIRS SALON FEATURES A GALLERY OF PORTRAITS
OF THE RUSPOLI FAMILY'S ANCESTORS, THE MARESCOTTI OF BOLOGNA.
THEY WERE DESCENDANTS OF MARIO LO SCOTTO, HEAD OF THE SCOTTISH TROOPS
WHO FOUGHT ALONGSIDE THE ARMIES OF CHARLEMAGNE.

case. According to documents from the Ruspoli archive, the garden was probably laid out around 1612, after the death of Ottavia's husband Marc Antonio.)

Still, it is not known if Ottavia was solely responsible for the entire garden, which includes a *giardino segreto* (secret garden) and a terrace leading to a *barco*, both of which are now under restoration. Ruspoli hopes that, with a recent grant from the European Union, she will be able to uncover a maze of grottoes and labyrinths that were once among the garden's other prominent features.

While Ottavia bequeathed to Italy one of its most enchanting gardens, many visitors to the Ruspoli Castle come away even more impressed by the life of her daughter Giacinta Marescotti. Although she had fallen in love and wished to marry, her family opposed her and instead sent her to the convent in Viterbo. In time, her former suitor married her younger sister. Feeling embittered and betrayed, for the next seventeen years, Giacinta lived a life of confined luxury and, some even say, depravity. Only after a near-fatal illness was she inspired to mend her ways, and dedicate her life to penitence and charitable works.

"Her chief accomplishment was to convince the leading brigand of the day, Francesco Pacini, to give up his nefarious ways and become her good

IN THE RED SALON
HANGS A FULL-LENGTH PORTRAIT OF PRINCE FRANCESCO RUSPOLI,
THE FRIEND AND PATRON OF THE COMPOSER HANDEL.
ON THE CONSOLE TO THE LEFT
IS A BUST OF THE GREAT-GRANDFATHER OF CLAUDIA RUSPOLI,
ALESSANDRO RUSPOLI,
WHO WAS A PAPAL MASTER OF CEREMONIES.

right hand," says Ruspoli. "With his help she founded the first social orders of that time, the Sacconi and the Oblati di Maria devoted to the Virgin Mary. During the plague, she encouraged people from wealthy families to dress in hooded robes and assist poor people in the neighboring towns."

Continually eager to do penance for her sins, Giacinta decided that her body should be flayed with whips made of hemp or leather, the latter studded with tiny nails. "She wanted to relive the pain and suffering of Christ, and sometimes went to the point of hanging from an enormous cross in her convent cell," recalls Ruspoli. "At other times, she would walk all night in the snow in her bare feet, repeating aloud the Stations of the Cross."

In 1807 Giacinta was made a saint; a glass case inside the castle's private chapel retains her simple brown habit, along with some of her letters, prayer books, reliquaries, and the whips that she used for self-flagellation.

While it cannot be easy to recall all this history, Principessa Claudia Ruspoli appears to wear it lightly and with good humor. "I receive more and more requests from people who wish to visit the castle and the garden. Sometimes, they're from the concierge at the Grand Hotel, who asks me to expect four people—not just for a tour, but also for lunch!" While lunch is not on the agenda of this unusual hostess, visitors are bound to delight in the friendly and informative welcome at the castle of Vignanello, with its enchanting, lemon-scented garden and its trove of spellbinding stories of the Ruspolis and the Marescottis.

THE CASTLE'S ANCIENT WELL
AND THE BAPTISMAL FONT
FROM THE
PARISH CHURCH OF VIGNANELLO,
CAN BE SEEN
THROUGH THE DOORWAY LEADING
TO THE PRIVATE CHAPEL.

Galleria Corsini d'Arte Antica a Palazzo Corsini

The National Gallery of Classical Art in the Corsini Palace

Via della Lungara, N. 10
Rome 00165
Tel: 06/688–02323

Open Tuesday through Friday
9:00 A.M. to 7:00 P.M.
Open Saturday 9:00 A.M. to
2:00 P.M.
Open Sunday and holidays
9:00 A.M. to 1:00 P.M.
Closed January 1, May 1, and
December 25.

Bus: 23, 44, 75, 170, 280, 717

THE PALAZZO CORSINI,
ONE OF THE MOST
DISTINGUISHED WORKS BY
THE ARCHITECT FERDINANDO FUGA,
WAS BUILT BETWEEN
1732 AND 1736 FOR
THE FAMILY OF POPE CLEMENT XII,
ON THE SITE OF
THE OLD RIARIO PALACE.

IT is a revelation to discover that one of Rome's most interesting palaces, which contains an outstanding collection of Hellenistic, Renaissance, and Baroque art, appears to be one of the city's most under-visited museums. Known as the National Gallery of Classical Art in the Corsini Palace, it is a stone's throw from the Porta Settimiana (one of the gates inside the Aurelian Wall), and directly across the street from the Villa Farnesina. Overlooking Rome's Botanical Garden, the palace exudes an aura of tranquillity, which is perhaps why it now houses the Accademia Nazionale dei Lincei, founded by Prince Federico Cesi in 1603 for the promotion of learning. (Galileo was a Lincean.)

Given the palace's tumultuous history, it is all the more remarkable that much of the gallery's painting, sculpture, and furniture collection has remained virtually intact. In 1797, a riot broke out near the palace between sympathizers of the French Revolution and the papal dragoons. In the ensuing battle, numerous shots were fired and the French General Duphot was killed. Duphot's death was all the pretext General Louis-Alexandre Berthier needed to launch an assault on Rome and organize the extradition of Pope Pius VI, who died the following year in France.

In 1849, when Napoleon III's troops breached the Janiculum walls (this time in support of the Pope), in an effort to defeat Garibaldi's fledgling Italian Republic, part of Trastevere found itself on the front line, and the back of the palace was

THIS IS THE ROOM WHERE QUEEN CHRISTINA LIVED
AND IS SAID TO HAVE DIED IN 1689.
THE PORTRAIT OF *QUEEN CHRISTINA OF SWEDEN AS DIANA*
BY JUSTUS VAN EGMONTS HANGS ON THE REAR WALL.

significantly damaged.

Thanks to a handsome restoration campaign, one may once again admire the palace's long and graceful façade designed by Ferdinando Fuga (1699–1781) and built between 1732 and 1736 for the Viceroy of Sicily, Bartolomeo Corsini, and his brother

Cardinal Neri, nephews of the ruling Pope Clement XII. Using the site of the old Riario Palace (which he transformed into a wing of the new edifice), Fuga created a huge open atrium with a triple barrel vault centered around a double-staircase, which is regarded as one of the most majestic and beautiful in Rome.

The Riario Palace was the home of Queen Christina of Sweden and, before that, of Caterina Sforza, who came to live here after her marriage to

THE MARBLE BUST OF CLEMENT XII
BY THE SCULPTOR
PIETRO BRACCI (1700–1773)
IS NOTABLE FOR ITS LIVELY REALISM.

Girolamo Riario in 1477. Although at that time, Caterina was at the height of her beauty—which was said to "glow like the sun and rival the lilies"—she had the misfortune of incurring the Borgias' wrath. In 1500 she returned to Rome as Cesare Borgia's prisoner and was incarcerated in the Castel Sant' Angelo. She might

have died there if the Borgias' French allies had not admired her greatly and insisted upon her liberation.

After Queen Christina converted to Catholicism and abdicated the Swedish throne, she moved to Rome in 1655. Eventually she took up residence at the Riario Palace, which she filled with her art collection and turned into a center of intellectual ferment. One of the leading artistic patrons of her epoch, she employed Scarlatti as her chapelmaster and Corelli as the director of her orchestra. Much to the pontiff's chagrin, she was no compliant Catholic, developing an interest in alchemy and astronomy, as well as in erotic art.

Visitors are often surprised to learn that the wealthy Corsinis not only assembled this enviable art collection, but also contributed to Rome's architectural and cultural heritage. Among their accomplishments were laying out the Piazza di Trevi and commissioning the Trevi Fountain, founding two museums (the Capitoline and the Calcografia), and building the principal façade of St. John Lateran.

Inside the palace atrium and lining the staircases are a group of ancient Roman sarcophagi and Hellenistic portrait busts, mainly from the second and third centuries A.D. Not to be overlooked on the right staircase is the famous sarcophagus of the *Sea Thiasos,* said to have inspired the statues of the Trevi Fountain.

The upper vestibule contains a group of mostly nineteenth-century Neoclassical statues, almost all of which come from the destroyed Torlonia Palace in Piazza Venezia, including those of Antonio Canova and John Gibson, Canova's pupil. Gibson is best remembered for tinting his statues (some say with tobacco juice), a realistic touch that shocked the puritanical sensibilities of such visiting New Englanders as Nathaniel Hawthorne.

Wishing to honor the memory of Queen Christina of Sweden, the Corsinis insisted that Fuga leave unchanged the room where she had died in 1689. Cardinal Neri commissioned the restoration of the vault's late-sixteenth-century frescoes illustrating the stories of Moses and Solomon and replaced the Riario coat-of-arms with his own. Although Justus van Egmonts' (1601–1674) painting of *Queen Christina of Sweden as Diana* has center-stage, the most striking artworks in this room are the still-lifes by Christian Berentz (1658–1722): *Still-life: The Clock* and *Still-life: The Fine Snack.* The Hamburg-born artist was an innovator in this genre—the precision of his fine lines and the crystal-like clarity of his objects exalt the harmonious nature of reality, in marked contrast to the Italian Baroque's opulence.

The gallery devoted to Tuscan primitive paintings includes an admirable Triptych by Fra "Beato" Angelico (1400–1455), depicting the *Last Judgment, the Ascension, and the Pentecost,* the only fifteenth-century work acquired by the Corsinis in the eighteenth century for the derisory sum of 30 scudi. This jewel-like work can be dated to the same time that Fra Angelico worked on the Vatican's Nicholas V chapel. An artist who knew the silence of the cloister, and who never picked up a brush without first making a prayer, Fra Angelico expressed his intense faith by painting serene and saintly faces, as well as a Christ who inspires adoration.

So impressed was Giorgio Vasari by this painter's work that he wrote: "In their bearing and expression, the saints painted by Fra Angelico come nearer to the truth than the figures done by any other artist. He would never retouch or correct his pictures, leaving them always just as they had been painted since that, as he used to say, was how God wanted them."

Among the outstanding works from the sixteenth-century Italian school is Fra Bartolommeo's (1472–1517) *Holy Family,* painted in Florence and praised by Vasari in his writings on the artist. Once used as a private altarpiece in the Doni family chapel, where it remained until it was purchased by Cardinal Neri, this monumental, pyramid-shaped

THE BUST-LINED VESTIBULE FEATURES NEOCLASSICAL SCULPTURES BY JOHN GIBSON, ANTONIO SOLA, AND PIETRO TENERANI.

painting recalls the invigorating dynamism of Michelangelo's later years in Rome. Vasari credits Bartolommeo's mastery over the human anatomy partially to the fact that he often worked with a life-size wooden model made with moveable joints and clothed in drapery.

The collection also underscores the

important influence of the master of tenebrism, Michelangelo Merisi da Caravaggio (1573–1610). His *Saint John the Baptist in the Desert*, painted in 1606, is endowed with an intense luminosity. The painting's raking light emphasizes the saint's youthful body scorched by the sun, thus creating dense areas of darkness and obscure recesses from which everyday objects and the roots of trees glimmer mysteriously. Despite his problems with the ecclesiastical establishment, which castigated him for his realism, Caravaggio's influence on painting was to last for generations. The outstanding Caravaggesque paintings in this collection that deserve special mention include Gerard Seghers' *Judith and Holophernes,* and Simon Vouet's *Herodias.*

THIS PAINTING BY JOSE RIBERA,
VENUS DISCOVERING THE DEAD BODY OF ADONIS (SIGNED AND DATED 1637),
IS ONE OF THE ARTIST'S MASTERPIECES,
REFLECTING THE INFLUENCE OF THE NEAPOLITAN NEO-VENETIANISM
THAT HAD BECOME WIDESPREAD IN ROME.

Following the advice of Giovanni Gaetano Bottari, an eminent scholar and one of the founders of modern art history, Cardinal Neri added many classical works to the collection— a move which required an intense and dedicated reconsideration of the whole Italian Baroque tradition.

Reflecting a return to the serene and noble style of Raphael and the Carracci (as opposed to the more florid and dramatic style of Pietro da Cortona), these Classically-inspired artists chose pagan or Biblical themes replete with moral intent. This artistic movement was led by Andrea Sacchi (1599–1661), his pupil Carlo Maratta (1625–1713), and Nicolas Poussin (1594–1665), all of whom are represented in this collection. Among the most beautiful works from this period is Maratta's *Rebecca at the Fount,* notable for its subtle psychological

drama: painted in glowing colors, it is reminiscent of the work of Venetian painters from a century earlier.

With the unification of Italy and the altered status of the Papal States, the Corsinis' interest in the palace dwindled, and after the death of Prince Tommaso Corsini, the family decided to return definitively to Florence. Fortunately, in 1883, the new Italian government of Zanardelli chose to raise the necessary funds to acquire the Corsini Palace and its collections, rather than risk their dispersion and sale overseas. Thanks to this far-sighted initiative, the fortunate visitor can now spend hours of pleasurable discovery amid one of the truly unique art collections in Rome.

The Doria Pamphilj Gallery

Piazza del Collegio Romano, N. 2
Rome 00186
Tel: 06/797–323

Open every day except Thursday
10:00 A.M. to 5:00 P.M.
Closed all major holidays,
including Christmas, New Year's
Day, and Easter.

Bus: 56, 60, 64, 70, 85, 87, 94, 95

IT'S not often that a man gives up a political position that is equivalent to secretary-of-state in order to marry and devote his life to amassing an extensive and impressive art collection. Yet, that is exactly what Prince Camillo Pamphilj chose to do when he gave up his appointment as *cardinal nipote* (the root word for "nepotism"), in order to marry the beautiful and wealthy Olimpia Aldobrandini in 1647. Nor did his unorthodox decision go over well with his uncle, Pope Innocent X; in fact, the Pope was so furious that he banished the couple from Rome for several years.

Still, after spending many enthralled hours inside the splendid state and private apartments of the Doria Pamphilj Gallery off Via del Corso, contemplating an art collection that boasts over 700 paintings and sculptures alone, one is compelled to believe that Camillo's decision was not only judicious, but even downright admirable.

From the moment one walks up the sweeping stone staircase, whose landing is set off by an imposing marble portrait bust, and enters the first state apartment known as the Poussin Room, where every inch of wall space is covered with large seventeenth-century landscape paintings, most of which are by Gaspar Dughet (Nicolas Poussin's brother-in-law), one cannot help but feel overwhelmed. With its double row of floor-to-ceiling windows, its ceiling painted with the Pamphilj coat of arms and such allegorical scenes as *Time Discovers Truth* and *Merit Crowns Virtue,* not to mention its

AS BEFITS A PRINCELY FAMILY,
THE ENTRANCE HALL
IS DECORATED WITH ASSORTED
ROMAN BUSTS AND STATUES,
AS WELL AS THE DORIA PAMPHILJ CREST
OVER THE DOOR.

THE THRONE ROOM WAS BUILT SPECIFICALLY FOR PAPAL VISITS.
WHENEVER THE POPE VISITED THE PALACE,
HE WOULD IMMEDIATELY BE SHOWN INTO A ROOM WHERE HE COULD RECEIVE HIS HOSTS.
BENEATH THE CANOPY HANGS A PORTRAIT OF INNOCENT X,
THE ONLY POPE IN THE PAMPHILJ FAMILY.

UNIFORMED "GUARDS" WATCH OVER A RARE EIGHTEENTH-CENTURY HARP
AND AN ORNATE BIRDCAGE DECORATED WITH PAPAL ARMS AND CHERUBS FOR SUPPORTS.
THE TWO DOVES THAT WERE PLACED INSIDE THE CAGE—SYMBOLS OF
PEACE AND THE HOLY SPIRIT—WERE RELEASED DURING CANONIZATION CEREMONIES.

BEHIND THE LAVISHLY CARVED AND GILDED CEREMONIAL CRADLE
IS A GOBELINS TAPESTRY DEPICTING THE MONTH OF DECEMBER
FROM A SERIES ON THE MONTHS OF THE YEAR BY PIERRE-FRANCOIS COZETTE.

flamboyant red velvet-covered settees and chairs, and red marble-topped gilded wood consoles, the room is a study in bravura. Even if Camillo had decided to relinquish a certain kind of temporal power, he still wanted visitors to be suitably impressed with his position and wealth, as well as with the scope of his collection. He needn't have worried.

Visitors used to current museum installations, which generally tend to be well-lit and systematically organized, may be a bit taken aback by the profusion of works of art throughout the gallery and the lack of identifying labels. "During the seventeenth and eighteenth centuries, works of art were treated as elements in an overall decorative scheme, and patrons like Camillo commissioned works of art to fill every visible inch of wall space," notes Prince Jonathan Pamphilj, whose family still lives in the palace and who had a major role in the gallery's refurbishing in 1996. "We have wanted to remain true to the original spirit of the collection."

THE GALLERY OF MIRRORS
WAS DESIGNED BY GABRIELE VALVASSORI BETWEEN 1731 AND 1734.
THE PRESENT ARRANGEMENT,
ALTERNATING GILT-FRAMED MIRRORS WITH HEAVILY RESTORED ANTIQUE STATUES,
WAS COMPLETED BY FRANCESCO NICOLETTI AROUND 1750
AND DECORATED WITH MONOCHROME *TROMPE-L'OEIL* EMBELLISHMENTS
BY GIOVANNI ANGELONI AND PIETRO BERNABO IN 1769.

(Nonetheless, to enhance the viewing pleasure of visitors, the gallery provides a multilingual audioguide that highlights not only the history of the collection, but draws attention to many of its outstanding pieces.)

Another unexpected surprise is the canopied Throne Room, first installed in 1760, when the palace became the principal family residence. "The throne was for the Pope," explains Prince Pamphilj. "When the Pope came to visit he would immediately be shown to a room where he would receive you—you couldn't receive him. His portrait would hang under the canopy, and in this case, we have hung a portrait of Innocent X, who was uncle to Prince Camillo."

Noting that the gilded throne, the only chair with cut velvet on both front and back, is turned backward to face the papal portrait beneath a matching cut-velvet canopy, Pamphilj suggests that this might be a throwback to the days when certain aristocratic families turned the throne to the wall as a protest against the Pope's being driven from the Papal States during the unification of Italy in 1870. "But as our family has always been supportive of the Italian state, my mother, Princess Doria Pamphilj, is horrified that we could have ever done such a thing." In fact, Filippo Andrea IV, noted for his moral probity and stance against Fascism, was elected Mayor of Rome following the city's liberation in 1944.

No single object in this palace better underscores the family's position than the grandiose carved and gilded wood intaglio ceremonial cradle in the Red Room, which was built to hold the new heir, shortly after the branches of the Doria and Pamphilj family were joined in 1761. It is all the more fitting that overhead is a ceiling fresco of *Jacob's Dream* by Pietro Angeletti (1737–1798), suggesting that the family's wish to have a line of descendants as long as that of the biblical patriarch was to be granted.

THE MARBLE BUST OF INNOCENT X BY GIAN LORENZO BERNINI REVEALS A MAN OF GREAT RESERVE AND DIGNITY. YET THE CREASES IN HIS MOZZETTA AND THE BUTTON LEFT ONLY HALF-BUTTONED ALSO SHOW THE POPE'S VULNERABILITY.

By a great coup, the proud parents, Andrea IV and Leopoldina di Savoia, were able to secure both the Pope and the Austrian Emperor Joseph II as the child's godparents, and it seems this cradle was used to commemorate the event. "Fortunately, my sister and I never had to lie in such a thing!" mirthfully exclaims Pamphilj.

Without a doubt the most sumptuous part of the palace is the four-sided picture gallery overlooking the inner courtyard and gardens, whose contents were reordered starting in 1766 under the supervision of Francesco Nicoletti, a talented but little-known architect, who cultivated a close association between painting and the decorative arts.

"By then the art collection had grown to over six hundred artworks," notes Pamphilj. "When we found Nicoletti's plans in our family archives, we were able to re-create the eighteenth-century style gallery you see here today. Everything was calculated so precisely, that we had to use a computer program in order to find where to put the nails in the wall so we could fit in all the pictures."

Pamphilj is persuaded that Nicoletti sometimes juxtaposed different paintings as a form of social commentary. To support this supposition, he notes that an anonymous seventeenth-century Genoese painting showing a rather corpulent cook surrounded by a kitchen filled with every conceivable food is deliberately placed on the same wall as an emaciated *Saint Paul the Hermit* by Pasquale Chiesa. "No curator would conceive of making such a juxtaposition today," he maintains.

What is also notable about this highly personal collection is its revelation of the extent to which formidable members of the Pamphilj family inspired some of the finest masterpieces in Baroque art. Take the strikingly powerful portrait bust of Olimpia Maidalchini Pamphilj by Alessandro Algardi (1598–1654). She was the wife of Pamphilio Pamphilj, as well as the lover of his brother Giovanni Battista (the man she ruthlessly propelled to become Innocent X). Algardi captured her willful nature which earned her the name "La Papessa," at a time when she was the real power behind the papal throne. Not only did she convince Innocent X that it was immoral for the Vatican to collect taxes from houses of prostitution, but she succeeded in getting him to sell her the license to collect these taxes for herself and her family!

However, when foreign dignitaries began visiting her before going to see the Pope, Innocent X decided that enough was enough, and banished her from the papal court. Only just before his death were they reconciled. "She must have been a nightmare to live with," notes her descendant ruefully. "Yet the fortunes of my family are due, in good part, to her."

While the Pamphilj collection contains works by Memling, Tempesta, Domenichino, Bassano, Raphael, Il Guercino, Titian, Caravaggio, Pieter Brueghel the Elder, David Teniers the Younger, Claude Lorrain, and Bernini, its most famous painting is indubitably the portrait of Innocent X by Diego Velázquez (1599–1660), painted around 1650 after the Spanish artist came to Rome for the Holy Year. A dramatic study in red, brocade, and velvet, the artist exposes the frowning ugliness of his sitter, an expression which engendered the suspicion among the Pope's enemies that he had a narrow and despotic temperament. Velázquez's mastery as a painter yielded him twenty more commissions in Rome after this work was completed, although Innocent's reaction showed that he was startled, at best. "Troppo vero!" he cried, upon seeing it. ("It's too real!")

Adjacent to this monumental work is Gian Lorenzo Bernini's unforgettable marble bust of Innocent X. While the artist's ceremonial bust emphasizes the sitter's dignity and stature, he also reveals the Pope's humanity in his gaunt and time-worn face, in the creases in his cloak, even in one of his half-buttoned buttons. "Sadly, Innocent X never chose to make use of the man many consider to have been the greatest sculptor

FORMERLY THE MUSIC ROOM,
THE BALLROOM UNDERWENT A COMPLETE REDECORATION
AT THE END OF THE NINETEENTH CENTURY.
ITS CEILING FRESCO CELEBRATES THE MARRIAGE BETWEEN
THE DORIA AND THE PAMPHILJ FAMILIES.
THE ROOM'S ORNATE CRYSTAL SCONCES WERE FORMERLY ILLUMINATED
WITH PLATINUM FILAMENT BULBS,
WHICH GAVE OFF A SOFT, BEAUTIFUL LIGHT.

who ever lived," notes Pamphilj. "It was because of his association with Pope Urban VIII, who was a member of the Barberini family. At his election Innocent X condemned the Barberinis for bankrupting the papal treasury and, as punishment, seized their palaces. As the Barberinis' favorite artist, Bernini also fell out of favor."

Unlike his uncle, Camillo Pamphilj never let politics or local feuds get in the way of his own aesthetic discernment. It was moving to learn that this independent-minded patron took pains to acquire two early works by Michelangelo Caravaggio, *Rest During the Flight into Egypt* and *The Penitent Magdalen*, when the artist's personal and professional reputation was at a particular low. These masterful paintings, which amply demonstrate Caravaggio's innovative realism and flair for the dramatic, are two more reasons to visit the Doria Pamphilj Gallery, an exceptional collection that offers hours of amusing and dazzling discoveries.

Mostra Permanente di Carrozze

The Permanent Exhibition of Carriages

Via A. Millevoi, N. 693
Rome 00178
Tel: 06/507–3500

Open Tuesday through Friday,
3:30 P.M. to 7:30 P.M.
Open Saturday and Sunday
9:30 A.M. to 1:30 P.M. and
3:30 P.M. to 7:30 P.M.

Bus: 702

T H E earliest and simplest carriage used by ancient peoples was the chariot, first employed by the Babylonians around 2000 B.C. Prior to the introduction of horses, this primitive conveyance had been drawn by asses. When the chariot and the horse were introduced into Egypt by the Hyksos invaders around 1700 B.C., they not only contributed to the military successes of these warriors but also spurred other peoples in the Middle East to adopt the vehicle as a war machine.

In the Hellenistic world, the chariot was never used to any great extent in war; instead it occupied a prominent place in games and processions. It was in Rome that

THE CHARIOT USED IN THE MOVIE *BEN-HUR* IS SIMILAR TO THE CHARIOTS THAT THE ETRUSCANS INTRODUCED INTO ITALY.

THIS SICILIAN CARRIAGE, FILLED WITH A CRATE OF LOVELY LEMONS, IS DECO-
RATED WITH EIGHTEENTH-CENTURY FOLK ART.

circus chariot races first developed. This ancient chariot was a very light vehicle, drawn by two or more horses hitched side by side. The car itself was little more than a floor with a waist-high semicircular guard in front.

While there are no ancient chariots left in existence, visitors to the Permanent Exhibition of Carriages will be able to admire the most famous chariot to have come out of Hollywood, the one which had a starring role in *Ben-Hur's* chariot race. A light wagon, used for races as well as for war, it could harness two or more horses. The chariot's box rested above two wheels, so that in the tightened bends the wagon wouldn't easily overturn. The back was open so that the person standing next to the charioteer could mount without difficulty and jump out more quickly during a race, a design that was later adapted for streetcars.

Although *Ben-Hur's* chariot never fails to impress visitors, it is only one of over a hundred unusual horse-drawn vehicles on display in this atypical 3,000-square-meter exhibition hall located inside a modern housing development in the Ardeatine section of Rome. The brainchild of entrepreneur and real estate developer Romoli Appolloni, this underground museum claims to have the most complete collection of carriages and coaches in existence.

Many of these vehicles have been equipped with life-size horses and donkeys, illustrating these animals'

AN ITALIAN OMNIBUS AND AN AMERICAN COVERED-WAGON
SHOW HOW HORSE-DRAWN VEHICLES COULD BE ADAPTED FOR EITHER
URBAN TRANSPORTATION OR CROSS-COUNTRY TREKS.

vital role in the transportation of both goods and men. This museum is of particular appeal to children, who are able to climb into the handsomely restored coaches, and imagine what it must have been like to ride in a horse-drawn vehicle and perhaps face such trials as getting stuck in muddy ruts after the rain, racing against time to deliver goods and mail, and braving the assaults of highway robbers.

Describing his passion for these horse-drawn vehicles as "an adventure" which began by chance forty years ago with the purchase of a horse-drawn carriage once used to transport tourists around the main sites of Rome, Appolloni counts examples from almost every era and nation in his collection, ranging from the European continent to North America and Asia. The variety of vehicles is just as vast, including a Danish winter sleigh, an Italian hearse, a colorfully painted farm wagon from Apulia, and the German landau once used by Pope John Paul II during his Polish episcopate (not to mention the Irish wagon driven by the actor John Wayne in *The Quiet Man*).

While Roman road-building encouraged the development of the horse-drawn vehicle, after the fall of the Empire horses and litters were used exclusively until the twelfth century, when carts and wagons were gradually reintroduced as modes of transportation.

The closed four-wheeled carriage, with two inside seats and an elevated outside seat for the driver, is believed to have been developed in Hungary and to have spread among royalty and the nobility during the sixteenth century. "The most ancient factory making carriages originated in Hungary in the city of Kotze," notes Appolloni. "The name of the town was distorted into the word 'coche,' from which is derived the word 'coach.' "

Milan, Naples, and Ferrara were the first Italian cities to import carriages from Hungary. While these carriages were introduced gradually into other European countries, in Italy they became popular very quickly. Between the second half of the sixteenth century and the second half of the seventeenth century, Italy

AMONG THE ELABORATE RIDING ACCESSORIES ARE AN
ARABIAN SADDLE (FAR LEFT),
AND A TURKISH SADDLE (SECOND FROM RIGHT).

became the leading manufacturer of carriages. In fact, there was such competition among aristocratic and bourgeois families as to who could own the most elaborate horse-drawn vehicles, that the popes were forced to pass sumptuary laws to restrain the worst excesses.

With the French Revolution, the principle of equality influenced fashion and customs to such an extent that carriage-makers were forced to adapt them to the needs of the middle-class. Judging by the carriages in this exhibition, excess luxury was abandoned in favor of comfort and speed. It was the right time for the introduction of the *landau* (first made in Landau, Germany), an elegant four-wheeled, two-seated carriage with a top in two parts which could be closed over or folded back depending upon the weather. Other notable carriages from this period were the *vis-à-vis* (a carriage for two that permitted socializing); the *berlin* (an elegant carriage for long-distance trips, named after its city of origin); the *cabriolet* (which contributed to an improved rapidity in postal communications); and the *coupé* or *berlinetta,* a closed carriage with windows on all sides and two seats, which could be drawn by one horse or a pair.

The most sumptuous carriage in the entire collection has to be the *berlinetta* for children that was originally made for Princess Sissi of Austria. Painted almost entirely in red and gold, except for its doors, which are decorated with enchanting landscapes, it's the sort of carriage that a fairy godmother might have procured for a princess.

At the opposite end of the spectrum is the *omnibus* (the word comes from Latin, meaning the "bus for all"). This was born from an idea devised by the seventeenth-century philosopher and mathematician Blaise Pascal (1623–1662), to put at public disposal carriages that would make the same trip every day from one district to another in Paris. These horse-drawn streetcars (which were originally built in France), could carry eighteen people on benches arranged longitudinally along the sides of the carriage. Unlike other carriages for hire, the omnibus allowed passengers to descend at any point along the route. In 1845, the omnibus was enlarged to carry up to twenty-six people, and this expanded carriage was drawn by three horses harnessed to two shafts. By the end of the nineteenth century, major cities such as London, Paris, Berlin, and New York, boasted double-decker omnibuses, which are now recognized as the precursor of the double-decker bus.

Carriages were such a critical factor in transportation in the nineteenth century that statesmen became involved in their development. In 1850, the English minister Lord Brougham (1778–1868) ordered the Robinson factory to build a four-wheeled, box-like closed carriage with an exterior perch for the driver that was eventually named after him. Seeing the museum's elegant white Italian *brougham,* with its tufted velvet banquette and two gleaming glass-and-brass headlights, one can understand how this type of vehicle later inspired the first automobiles, which were powered by an electric motor.

The *caravan,* a canvas-covered wagon (which originated in Pennsylvania), was used as a house on wheels, and was intended to hold enough provisions, weapons, ammunition, and drinking water for long and arduous trips. Its unusually wide spoke wheels enabled the pioneers to move across rocky terrain with greater ease, which is likely why this vehicle played such a significant role in

THIS LAVISH AUSTRIAN CARRIAGE FOR CHILDREN, A *BERLINETTA*,
WAS ONCE USED BY "SISSI,"
THE HUNGARIAN PRINCESS ELIZABETH OF AUSTRIA.

settling America's western states, particularly Colorado and California. Knowing that such vehicles offered scant refuge from harsh weather and storms, one cannot help but admire the courage and resolve of the settlers who drove them.

The collection also features a number of versions of the *victoria*, a vehicle aptly named after Queen Victoria, who preferred this carriage above all others because of its wide and comforting shape and excellent suspension system, which was adaptable to almost any road. Built in both two-seat and four-seat models, it could be drawn by one or two horses. "Although this carriage was appreciated by a woman, it wasn't disdained by men," observes

Appolloni. "In fact, in 1875, Victor Emmanuel II gave one to Giuseppe Garibaldi."

While enjoying this impressive collection of horse-drawn vehicles and accessories, the visitor is bound to be struck by the variety of ways this mode of transportation has marked every segment of society, as well as most corners of the globe. "This exhibition gives young people and their elders the possibility of knowing more about a means of transportation that is nowadays in disuse, but which certainly hasn't lost any of its charm or appeal," notes Appolloni. "We think this museum affords a unique occasion to rediscover these vehicles, which can tell us so much about our past."

Museo Archeologico Nazionale di Palestrina

The National Archaeological Museum of Palestrina

Palazzo Barberini
Piazza della Cortina
Palestrina (Rome) 00036
Tel: 06/953–8100

Open every day except Christmas, New Year's Day, and May 1 9:00 A.M. until one hour before sunset.
(If visiting the museum on public holidays, prior booking is required.)

By train: Leave from Zagarolo Station with COTRAL shuttle service to Palestrina.
By bus: Take the COTRAL motor coach departing from Rome from either the Anagnina or the Rebibbia subway stations.
By car: Take A24, exit Tivoli, Via Maremmana, Via Prenestina. A2, exit San Cesareo, ss155 for Fiuggi. A2, exit Val Montone, ss55/a Pedemontana 11.

An hour's drive east of Rome along the southern slope of Mount Ginestro lie the ancient ruins of the town of Praeneste, one of the oldest settlements in Latium, said to have been founded by Telegonus, the son of Ulysses and Circe, the latter famed for changing men into swine. From the second century B.C. until the fourth century A.D. pilgrims from all over the Roman Empire wended their way up its steep hillside to the Sanctuary of Fortuna Primigenia, whose oracle claimed to predict the future through a system of *sortes,* or lots, which consisted of pieces of wood upon which letters had been carved.

THE MUSEUM IS HOUSED IN A PALACE BUILT IN THE MIDDLE AGES AT THE TOP OF THE SANCTUARY OF FORTUNA PRIMIGENIA. ORIGINALLY A FORTRESS BELONGING TO THE COLONNA FAMILY, THE PALACE WAS REBUILT BETWEEN 1490 AND 1500, AND NOW FEATURES AN ELEGANT PORTAL AND SYMMETRICALLY ARRANGED WINDOWS.

At its zenith, this monumental sanctuary, built between 130 and 100 B.C., consisted of a series of six artificial terraces built into the hillside's rocky slope and connected by a series of ramps and staircases converging toward a temple honoring the Goddess of Fortune at the summit.

Regarded as the most majestic Hellenistic edifice in Italy, the sanctuary represents a breakthrough in the history of architecture, for it was one of the earliest recorded instances of the Roman use of concrete for a building's vaulting. (Because concrete had important static properties and was a less costly material than marble, it permitted the construction of enormous and daring buildings.)

Yet, neither archaeologists nor visitors would ever have known the scope of this ancient edifice and its multiple terraces, without the necessity of clearing the remains of buildings destroyed by the Allied bombing in 1944, which unearthed important elements of the renowned sanctuary. By the Middle Ages, a town called Citta Prenestina had been built over the abandoned sanctuary, but it was continuously subjected to conquests and takeovers. Not only was the town destroyed and rebuilt several times, its name was eventually changed to commemorate its most illustrious citizen, Giovanni Pierluigi da Palestrina (c. 1525–1594), the father of polyphonic music and the undisputed maestro of the Mass with 105 compositions to his name.

Today, the ruins and rich heritage of Praeneste can best be appreciated by a visit to the National Archaeological Museum of Palestrina, housed in the handsomely restored Medieval palace that still shows the traces of ceiling frescoes by the Zuccari brothers, late Italian Mannerist painters from Rome. As is true of so many edifices in Italy, the palace itself

THIS GALLERY,
WITH ITS RAVAGED CEILING FRESCOES
BY THE ZUCCARI BROTHERS,
ILLUSTRATES THE HELLENISTIC AGE
AT PRAENESTE,
WHEN THE CITY WAS A CENTER OF
INTENSE ARTISTIC ACTIVITY.
AMONG THE STATUES ON DISPLAY ARE
THREE HEADLESS WEALTHY
PRAENESTINE *MATRONAE* (MATRONS).

consists of layers of history: built in the Middle Ages at the top of the Sanctuary of Fortuna Primigenia, it was originally a fortress belonging to the Colonna family. About the middle of the fifteenth century, the building was radically transformed by closing off the portico of the former sanctuary and by adding a second floor. By 1500, the palace had been rebuilt to include the elegant portal and well that one sees today, while the windows were rearranged in symmetrical order. In 1630, Francesco Colonna sold the hillside town and the palace to Carlo Barberini, the brother of Pope Urban VIII, who remodeled it, adding the church of Santa Rosalia in 1660, where the *Pietà Barberini,* attributed to Michelangelo, was kept for a long time.

The elegant three-story museum uses a thematic and chronological arrangement and bilingual information panels (in Italian and English), to present some of the complex history of the cultural and artistic development of Praeneste and its intricate relations with Rome beween the Republican and Imperial eras.

The palace's massive stone walls and a system of newly installed fiber-optic lighting provide a dramatic backdrop against which to appreciate the museum's extensive collection of figurative and bas-relief sculpture, votive deposits from religious sanctuaries, as well as varied archaeological finds from nearby necropolises.

Thanks to an impressive assembly of epigraphic records (dedicatory inscriptions from tombstones and monuments), scholars have been able to document some of the political and military upheavals endured by the town of Praeneste, as well as corroborate the town's thriving economy when the Sanctuary of Fortuna Primigenia was in its prime.

In the last two decades of the second century B.C., Praeneste was the locale of intense artistic activity, due largely to the expenditures of a rich merchant class, which had gained considerable wealth through the Roman conquest of the East. It was this segment of society that provided the necessary financing to create the monumental sanctuary and renovate the town. Its members also had the means to induce Greek artists to migrate to Rome and its surrounding towns, where they were accorded both private and public commissions.

During the civil war in the first century B.C., Praeneste sided with General Gaius Marius (157 B.C.–86 B.C.). After Lucius Cornelius Sulla (138 B.C.–78 B.C.), leader of the

TOMBSTONES SHAPED LIKE PINE CONES AND SCULPTURES OF FEMALE PERSONAGES
REPRESENTING THE DECEASED WERE COMMON
IN THE NECROPOLIS OF PRAENESTE DURING THE THIRD AND SECOND CENTURIES B.C.

THE CAPITOLINE TRIAD OF MINERVA, JUPITER, AND JUNO
FROM THE ANTONINE AGE (A.D. 160–180) WAS RETRIEVED FROM THIEVES WHO WERE
ATTEMPTING TO TAKE IT OUT OF THE COUNTRY IN 1992.
MINERVA IS PORTRAYED WITH AN OWL, AND JUNO WITH A PEACOCK, WHILE JUPITER
IS SHOWN HOLDING A SCEPTER.

conservative senatorial party, defeated Gaius Marius and the Marians, he captured and massacred 8,000 prisoners, including members of the most distinguished families in Praeneste, who had built the sanctuary. Only women and children were spared.

While notorious for his reign of cruelty and illegality (the Senate ulimately forced him to resign in 79 B.C.), Sulla also used some of his ill-gotten war booty to lavish stupendous sums on the Sanctuary of Fortune at Praeneste. A steady influx of pilgrims to the temple spurred the growth of many professional associations (*collegia,* the root word for colleague), including metalworkers, wood and stonecutters, litter bearers, dyers, crown-makers, ceremonial flute-players, and butchers (who sold meat used in the sacrifices). The *collegia's* members used to meet for official dinners, commissioned dedications on stone memorial tablets offered to the god of each professional association, and were buried in corporate tombs, examples of which are in the museum. (While this professional structure disappeared with paganism, it laid the groundwork for the medieval guild system and later trade unions.)

Thanks to the excavations of the Colombella and Seliciata necropolises, which are nearby, visitors can now see how the dead were often buried with their personal possessions, including cylindrical beauty cases, known as *cists,* made of either copper or bronze, which were elaborately decorated and often filled with toiletry objects given to girls as wedding gifts.

While pride of place is given to the famed Capitoline Triad consisting of Jupiter flanked by Juno and Minerva (which used to be worshiped in the Temple of Jupiter on the Campidoglio), the museum also highlights the towering late Hellenistic black marble statue representing the union between the oracular Fortuna Primigenia and Isis, a maternal Oriental deity, whose cult took hold at Praeneste as early as the second century B.C.

A stunning collection of heads, busts, and full-length statuary representing both the realism of the Republican age and the idealization of the human form during the Imperial age, takes on an even greater significance thanks to the museum's illuminating explanation of the evolution of Roman sculpture.

THIS HEADLESS FEMALE FIGURE IS FROM PRAENESTE'S HELLENISTIC PERIOD, WHEN GREEK ARTISTS FROM THE EAST WERE COMMISSIONED TO CREATE SCULP-TURES FOR THE TOWN'S WEALTHY MER-CHANT CLASS.

Since the aristocracy in Republican Rome was the only social class per-mitted to exhibit their ancestors' por-traits at funerals and in the atrium of their homes, it was imperative that a portrait's rendering of a person's face should make that individual immedi-ately recognizable; in this way, the authorities could be sure that the family was acting within the strictures of the law. Only after Rome had conquered Greece and had become increasingly Hellenized did the idealization of the human form and heroic nudity take hold. Female statues were inspired by ideal models taken from the iconography of Greek gods and goddesses, as exemplified by three elaborately costumed statues in Greek marble of three wealthy Praenestine matrons.

The masterful technique of sculptors from the Augustan Age is best exemplified in the exquisitely detailed marble Grimani relief depicting a female boar suckling her young in a natural rocky environment rich in vegetation and wild flowers. Scholars believe the relief reflects not just the ideals of regeneration and propagation of the species, but also the period's widespread optimism brought about by the *Pax Romana,* a time of peace and prosperity through-out the Roman Empire. Just as impressive is the white marble bas-relief showing the triumphant proces-sion of an idealized Trajan advancing in a chariot drawn by four horses, a fine example of Imperial Rome's commemoration of a military victory.

While this elegant museum is filled with many outstanding pieces of sculpture and ancient artifacts, nothing prepares the first-time visitor for the museum's masterpiece, one of the most important extant Hellenistic mosaics from the second century B.C., depicting a wide prospective map of Egypt and the Nile flooding the land from its source in the mountains of Ethiopia to the delta on the Mediterreanean Coast. Originally used to decorate the rear apse floor of a large hall on the north side of Praeneste's Forum, the mosaic functions as both a geographical map and a natural history chart, with the

A DETAIL FROM THE *MOSAIC OF THE NILE*,
CREATED BY AN ALEXANDRIAN ARTIST
AT THE END OF THE SECOND CENTURY A.D.
IT WAS ONCE PART OF
THE PAVING OF A LARGE ROOM DEDICATED TO THE CULT OF ISIS,
LOCATED NEAR THE FORUM OF PRAENESTE.

mountains of Ethiopia in the upper portion, the City of Thebes and the Temple of Ammon in the center, and in the lower portion the Nile delta and the city of Memphis. River cataracts are contrasted with deserts, Egyptian warriors and a priestess stand before the Serapeum of Alexandria, while pygmies dance in a tropical forest inhabited by a variety of wild animals.

There can be no denying that it is a stupendous sight to behold, and only one of many that warrant a visit (and return visits) to the National Archaeological Museum of Palestrina.

Museo Nazionale di Arte Orientale

The National Museum of Oriental Art

Via Merulana, N. 248
(Palazzo Brancaccio)
Rome 00186
Tel: 06/487–4415

Open Monday, Wednesday,
Friday, and Saturday
9:00 A.M. to 2:00 P.M.
Tuesday and Thursday
9:00 A.M. to 7:00 P.M.
Sunday and holidays
9:00 A.M. to 1:00 P.M.
Closed first and third Monday
of the month.

Bus: 85, 87
Tram: 13

Two years after Rome was designated the capital of a newly united Italy, a wealthy New York grain merchant, Hickson Field, and his wife Mary E. B. Field, took advantage of the city's economic flux to acquire, for a comparatively modest sum, a vast stretch of land on the Oppian Hill overlooking the Colosseum that for centuries had belonged to the Abbey run by the Order of Santa Clara. The site was replete with history, for it concealed the ruins of Imperial Rome—Nero's Golden House and part of the Baths of Trajan.

However, the Fields were little

THE BRANCACCIO PALACE
WAS CONVERTED INTO THE NATIONAL MUSEUM OF ORIENTAL ART IN 1957.
BUILT BY LUCA CARIMINI FOR THE FIELD FAMILY
AT THE END OF THE NINETEENTH CENTURY,
ITS PROFUSE AND ELABORATE INTERIOR DECORATIONS WERE CONCEIVED, COORDINATED
AND, IN SOME CASES, EXECUTED BY FRANCESCO GAI, THE DIRECTOR OF
ST. LUKE'S ACADEMY IN ROME.

concerned at the time with the site's legendary reputation. Their aim was to commission a celebrated edifice of their own, a Roman residence befitting the recent marriage of their daughter Elizabeth to Prince Salvatore Brancaccio, a member of one of the oldest aristocratic Neapolitan families. Emulating the munificent art patrons of the Renaissance, the Fields turned to the architects Gaetano Koch and Luca Caramini to construct for them a palatial residence reflective of their newfound status, as well as their sizable fortune.

Although the Neo-Renaissance edifice and interior courtyard with its *Nympheum* are impressive to behold, the palace's fabulous stucco decoration and ceiling frescoes remain its chief attraction. Conceived and painted by the artist Francesco Gai (1835–1917), who was the director of St. Luke's Academy in Rome, the elaborate and whimsical decoration emulates Baroque and Rococo paintings, which capitalized on pagan myths to glorify a patron. One of the most striking examples of this decor is the ceiling fresco of *Venus Bathing* in the former bedroom of Princess Brancaccio.

These ornate interiors were hidden beneath sheetrock and plaster for decades, when the family's apartment was eventually transformed into the present National Museum of Oriental Art, which was inaugurated in 1957. Only when the museum underwent extensive refurbishing in 1991 were the original wall and ceiling decorations discovered.

The National Museum of Oriental Art, the most important institution devoted to Oriental art and archaeology in Italy, is regarded as the brainchild of Italy's leading twentieth-century Orientalist, Professor Giuseppe Tucci, an eminent scholar

THE STAIRCASE LEADING UP TO THE NATIONAL MUSEUM OF ORIENTAL ART REFLECTS THE GRANDIOSE TASTES OF THE PALACE'S FORMER OWNERS, ELIZABETH FIELD AND THE NEAPOLITAN PRINCE, SALVATORE BRANCACCIO.

of Oriental philosophy and religion at the University of Rome and at the University of Naples. His proficiency in languages and wide-ranging knowledge led him to undertake a trek that resulted in the discovery of the oldest known representations of Buddha in the Gandhara region of Pakistan's Swat Valley. "Through his readings in Chinese of seventh-century Buddhist pilgrims' accounts of their journey to this area, he was confident enough to organize an archaeological team to go there and set up scientific excavations in the Valley of Swat," notes curator Dr. Roberto Ciarla.

Originally a province of the Persian Empire, the Gandhara region was reached by Alexander the Great in 327 B.C. Under Kanishka, the King of Gandhara (c. A.D.120), who ruled

Hellenistic culture, including horses and chariots, Corinthian columns, and mythological figures.

"Gandharan art is important because it represents a fusion of Western art with Eastern philosophy," notes Mazzeo. "Yet at the same time, it was not created out of aesthetic considerations. Its ultimate aim was to stimulate prayer and meditation."

At this museum, visitors can follow the Buddhist faith's iconographic development from the earliest examples, as in Gandhara art, to eighteenth- and nineteenth-century interpretations of the Buddha in the different regions where the religion made inroads, including China, Mongolia, Tibet, Korea, Japan, and other parts of Southeast Asia. "You can see how in different cultural environments, the Buddha figure was interpreted in different ways," notes Ciarla. "At the same time, representations of Buddha had to conform to specific attributes; for instance he had to be shown with a topknot, have curly hair and long earlobes. Without these, and many other attributes, he would have been viewed as a false Buddha."

The Buddhist Tibetan art collection is one of the most important in Europe, thanks to Dr. Tucci's numerous journeys to Tibet and Nepal from the 1930s until the early 1950s. His fluency in Tibetan gave him unique access to the Dalai Lama, who befriended the Italian professor, and even gave him the honorary title of "Western Dalai Lama." In exchange for modern Western timepieces, the Dalai Lama gave Tucci 400 *tsa*, painted images of Buddhist saints molded in unbaked clay, which traveling monks took with them for protection, a splendid sixteenth-century fresco of Buddha from a defunct Tibetan monastery, and a collection of 150 fifteenth-to-nine-

over an empire that stretched from the Pamirs to Bengal, Buddhism flourished. Not only did this monarch encourage the spread of Buddhism to central Asia, but he also built many Buddhist monuments, known as *stupa,* and helped found a noted school of sculpture, consisting mainly of images of Buddha and reliefs representing scenes from Buddhist texts. "These Gandhara sculptures decorated the exterior of the *stupa,* which was said to contain sacred bones of the Buddha," explains Dott.ssa Donatella Mazzeo, the museum's director. "Pilgrims walked around the *stupa,* but never entered it."

Thanks to Professor Tucci's scientific and cultural exchanges with the Pakistan government, the museum possesses the largest collection of Gandhara art in Europe, dating from the first to the fourth century A.D. (The art form flourished until the fifth century, when the region was conquered by the Huns.) Sculpted out of blue-gray schist, the striking reliefs have marked Greco-Roman elements, including very realistic heads, finely chiseled features, flowing tunics, and features of teenth-century paintings on cloth, *tankhas* (made with natural pigments mixed with yak fat), which are used to stimulate meditation. (When *tankhas* are deemed too old, fresh ones are substituted. All the *tankhas* in the museum have lost their sacred aspect.)

The accepted convention that the fabric of Western civilization originated in the ancient city-states of the Middle East, is further confirmed by one of the museum's most significant finds—the remains of the five-thousand-year-old Shahr-e Sokhta (meaning the Burned City) that were brought to light in 1967 during an archaeological expedition conducted by the museum under the leadership of Professor Maurizio Tosi.

Although the area now represents one of the harshest deserts of Middle

THIS RARE SIXTEENTH-CENTURY ENCAUSTIC WALL PAINTING FROM WESTERN TIBET ILLUSTRATES A SCENE FROM THE LIFE OF BUDDHA.

THE GALLERY DEVOTED TO ISLAMIC ART FROM IRAN AND AFGHANISTAN
INCLUDES RARE SLIP-PAINTED VESSELS FROM THE SAMANID PERIOD
(NINTH AND TENTH CENTURIES A.D.),
HISPANO-MORESQUE LUSTERWARE, AND COLORFUL *KASHI* GLAZED TILES,
NAMED AFTER THE TOWN OF KASHAN.

Asia in Sistan (a large province in eastern Iran at the border of Pakistan and Afghanistan), between 3000 and 2000 B.C., Shahr-e Sokhta flourished along the Helmand River as an early Bronze Age agglomeration of peasants, herdsmen, craftsmen, and traders. (It is now widely believed that when the Helmand River evaporated, a thick crust of salt sealed and preserved intact the archaeological deposits.)

A display of ceramic vessels (mostly pear-shaped beakers decorated with painted animal motifs), alabaster vessels, turquoise, agate, and lapis beads, pendants, and seals, manufactured for local consumption and long-distance export, attest to a wealthy, sophisticated civilization, with multi-story housing, graves, copper foundries, pottery kilns, and jewelry ateliers, that had established a trading network

from Mesopotamia and the Indus Valley all the way to Central Asia.

Thanks to the dry climate, the deposit also yielded many organic materials now displayed in the museum, showing that the city's inhabitants had a meat-and-grain-based diet, wore clothes of woven wool and hemp, and used stone flints for cutting semi-precious stone beads and making wooden storage containers.

Although a collection of terracotta tablets covered with Proto-Elamite writing has yet to be deciphered, it is widely assumed that they were used in the Shahr-e Sokhta's economy and administration. "Hopefully, this exhibit will help visitors appreciate how long it has taken to progress from the early stages of private property to our current global economy,"

Ciarla notes.

The museum's comprehensive collection of Islamic art includes one of the most important archaeological finds, dating back to the twelfth century, which was excavated at the palace of King Mas'*ud* III (1099–1115) in Ghazni, a town southwest of Kabul, Afghanistan. The King was one of the rulers of the Ghaznavid dynasty (977–1186), a Turkish dynasty founded by a former Turkish slave, Sebüktigin, which—at its zenith under King Mahmud—had an empire stretching from present-day Afghanistan to a large portion of Persia and Northwest India. (It was Mahmud who converted the Ghaznavids from their pagan Turkic origins, and who expanded the frontiers of Islam.)

The dynasty's capital, Ghazni, became a city rich in palaces, monuments, and mosques; today, all that remains are the vestiges of Mas'*ud*'s palace and the basement of two minarets dating back to the twelfth century. Working with innovative architects, the Ghaznavids introduced the "four *eyvan*" ground plan into their palaces. (An *eyvan* is a large vaulted hall, enclosed on three sides and open to a court on the fourth.)

Cultural agreements between the former government of Afghanistan and the museum's archaeological team permitted excavations on the palace site in the early 1960s. These digs led to the unearthing of precious architectonic elements, including engraved marble slabs and baked bricks decorated with Kufic writing of verses from the Koran, as well as glazed tile-work, emulating the vegetal motifs and calligraphy used in Persian tapestries, which are unique finds in themselves. "The discovery of the palace represents one of the most important events in the history of Islamic archaeology," notes Ciarla. "It allowed us to enlarge our knowledge of ancient Islamic civilian architecture during the period preceding the sixteenth century."

Now, thanks to this museum's exceptionally imaginative scholarship and adventurous expeditions, the public has a unique opportunity to discover and contemplate the glorious diversity of Middle Eastern and Oriental art.

THE MUSEUM'S EXTENSIVE CHINESE ART COLLECTION IS DISPLAYED IN THE FORMER PRIVATE APARTMENT OF PRINCE BRANCACCIO, WHICH WAS DECORATED BY THE ROMAN PAINTER, FRANCESCO GAI.

Museo Barracco

The Barracco Museum

Piazza dei Baullari
Corso Vittorio Emanuele, N. 168
Rome 00186
Tel: 06/880–6848

Open Tuesday through Sunday
9:00 A.M. to 1:00 P.M.
Open Tuesday and Thursday
5:00 P.M. to 8:00 P.M.

Bus: 46, 62, 64, 110, 186

AN ANCIENT ROMAN COPY OF
THE APOLLO OF OMPHALOS,
EXCAVATED FROM CAESAR'S GARDEN
IN TRASTEVERE,
GREETS VISITORS TO THE
BARRACCO MUSEUM.

ONE of the most charming yet least visited Renaissance palaces in Rome, known as the Piccola Farnesina (mistakenly attributed to the Farnese family because of its decorative heraldic lilies), contains close to four hundred works of ancient Assyrian, Babylonian, Egyptian, and Greek sculpture—most of which are rarities, even in a city as cosmopolitan as Rome.

Amassed over the course of half a century by the wealthy and erudite Baron Giovanni Barrocco (1829–1914), the entire collection was bequeathed by its owner to the City of Rome in 1902. To accommodate the collection, Barrocco had commissioned the architect Gaetano Koch to design a museum that resembled an elegant Greek temple. All that remains of this Neoclassical edifice are photographs, since Mussolini's urban planning directives led to its destruction in 1938.

Yet, knowing Barrocco's passion for ancient archaeology, it is likely that he would not be disappointed in the collection's present location (open to the public since 1948). Beneath the palace's basement are the remains of a Roman building from the late Imperial period, which were discovered in 1899. Upon special request, visitors can view these Roman structures, which include a portico with fine columns and marble *opus sectile* flooring. Fragments of finely painted frescoes found among the building's remains (one fresco features a duck with a snake held in its beak, whereas another represents a deer hunt), are now displayed in the museum's library.

THIS HEADLESS FEMALE FIGURE IN PARIAN MARBLE
IS SHOWN POURING WATER FROM A VASE.
A HELLENISTIC WORK BROUGHT TO ROME, IT MOST LIKELY DECORATED
A FOUNTAIN AT ONE TIME.

The choice Egyptian sculpture includes some exceptional reliefs, including one that shows the pharaoh's scribe and treasurer Nofer, seated before a table laden with offerings. This stone relief (judging by its naïve style and raised hieroglyphics), was made during the Fourth Dynasty (c. 2778–2432 B.C.), thus making it the oldest Egyptian sculpture known in Rome.

The ancient Egyptians believed that it was not enough to preserve the body in a mummy case, but that the king's likeness should also be preserved, so that one could be doubly certain he would continue to exist forever. This is why sculptors were ordered to chisel the king's head out of immutable stone, and to place it in a tomb where no one would see it, since its sole purpose was to maintain the pharaoh's soul for the rest of eternity. No wonder one Egyptian

term for sculptor was *"he-who-keeps-alive."*

Among the museum's outstanding portrait heads, illustrating Egyptian mastery in this branch of art from 1500 B.C. through the Roman era, are two portraits in basalt of Ramses II, one as a child, the other as a helmeted young man, when he fought the Hittites and persecuted the Hebrews. After the Roman conquest of Egypt, these stone portraits became softer and less forbidding, judging by a green basalt head of a bearded priest, once mistaken for Julius Caesar. A painted golden stucco portrait from a woman's mummy case, notable for its dark, fixed gaze and elaborate headdress, illustrates the pervasive influence of Roman beauty and hairstyling during the Hellenistic period. The

gravity and simplicity of such works make them unforgettable, which is perhaps why this art had such a profound influence on such Modernists as Picasso and Matisse.

Although Egyptian art remained virtually unchanged for close to three thousand years, one monarch dared to challenge this style, Amenhotep IV, a king of the Eighteenth Dynasty's New Kingdom (c. 1500 B.C.), who ruled after a catastrophic invasion of Egypt. His portrait in profile can be admired on a polychrome stone fragment in the museum. Amenhotep recognized only one supreme deity, Aten, whom he worshiped, and represented as a sun disk—in fact, he called himself Akhenaten after his chosen god.

Yet, as remarkable as the portraits are, the museum's most significant Egyptian object may be a third-century B.C. black basalt *clepsydra* or a water clock , thought to have been invented during the Eighteenth Dynasty and later exported to Greece and Rome. This ancient device, which told time by the flow of water into a container, was reassembled from numerous fragments found in Rome's Campus Martius. The water clock's inner walls show some notches for measuring time, whereas its exterior is etched with hieroglyphics and a depiction of Ptolemy II of Philadelphia (now Amman, Jordan).

Because so few works of art have come down to us from Mesopotamia, the fragments of Assyrian bas-reliefs from the palaces of Nineveh and Nimrud are particularly valuable finds. These works are presumed to be from the ninth and eighth centuries B.C., slightly later than the reign of King Solomon. One relief, consisting of a stone slab from Ashurnasirpal II's northwest palace in Nimrud (c. 880 B.C.), represents a genius holding a pine cone in his right hand, a small

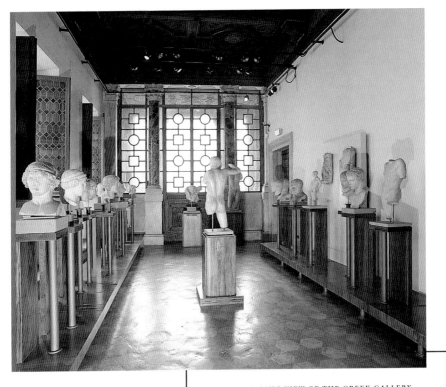

basket in his left. Another from King Sennacherib's southwest palace at Nineveh (704–681 B.C.) shows three warriors fleeing through a cane-field. While less precise and organized, both reliefs reveal the influence of Egyptian art.

Barrocco was especially concerned with numerous acquisitions representing the great Greek schools of the fifth and fourth centuries B.C. as well as with those from the Hellenistic period (end of the fourth through the first century B.C.). While it is a pity that almost no Greek originals from Phidias, Polycletus, and Myron have come down to us, Barracco's choice of copies was so fine that it is difficult to decide which ones to single out.

A white marble statue of Hermes Kriopheros carrying a ram on his shoulders (a copy of the bronze votive by Kalamis at Tanagra around 480 B.C.) is remarkable for its gentle countenance and grace, leading one to compare it with "the Good Shepherd," a paleo-Christian sculpture in the Vatican's Museo Cristiano. The head of an ephebe from the end of the sixth century B.C., with curly hair and a mysterious smile, and the portrait of a bearded Silenus Marsius, copied at the end of the fifth century from Myron's bronze masterpiece on the Acropolis, are equally striking.

Many will be drawn to the elegant portrayal of a young athlete that is likely a copy of a lost fifth-century B.C. work by Polycletus representing the boxer Kyniskos of Mantinea, which was dedicated to Olympia, the place where the ancient Olympic Games were held. Because the figure is missing its right arm, scholars have wondered whether the boxer is cleaning his body with a strigil, girding

THIS STATUE OF A GREEK YOUTH,
REPRESENTING A YOUNG ATHLETE,
IS A COPY OF AN ORIGINAL
BRONZE WORK BY POLYCLETUS.

copy of Lysippus's bronze), has to be one of the finest from ancient Rome. The Roman author Pliny mentions the bronze statue in his *Natural History,* noting that the bronze original was kept inside the Capitoline Temple of Jupiter, and that its custodians would be put to death if any harm should ever come to it.

Not to be missed is the small but fine collection of Roman sculpture. The acutely observed portraits are the most captivating of all, notably an exquisite portrait of a small boy (a young prince from the Julio-Claudian household found in Livia's Villa at Prima Porta), and a coolly elegant youth who lived during the reign of Tiberius.

In a city where there is comparatively little in the way of Medieval art, notably in mosaic, it comes as a pleasant surprise to find a fragment of a mosaic, depicting the figure of the *Ecclesia Romana,* that once was in the apse of the Old St. Peter's Basilica commissioned by Pope Innocent III (1198–1216). During

his head with a bandage, or assuming the crown of victory.

Although we are accustomed to rewarding and revering our finest athletes, the Greeks actually commissioned their leading sculptors to immortalize their sports champions in bronze and stone. In ancient Greece, a victor in the games was looked upon with awe as a man whom the gods had favored with the spell of invincibility. Scholars now maintain that sometimes the winners of these athletic contests (or their families) commissioned their own likenesses from renowned and accomplished artists, in order to consecrate and perhaps perpetuate these signs of divine favor.

While one can admire the beauty and power of this Greek athlete, as well as the portrait herms of *Homer* and a *Spearman,* a sculpture of the *Wounded Bitch* (said to be a marble

THIS ENGAGING PHOENICIAN LION,
MADE OF ALABASTER,
WAS DISCOVERED IN SARDINIA.

THIS THIRTEENTH-CENTURY MOSAIC OF THE *ECCLESIA ROMANA*
ONCE WAS PART OF THE APSE DECORATION OF ST. PETER'S BASILICA
THAT WAS COMMISSIONED BY POPE INNOCENT III.

the demolition of the apse's wall preceding Michelangelo's reconstruction of the Basilica in 1592, fragments of this mosaic were recovered, including this *Ecclesia Romana*. Yet, it remained largely unknown until Barrocco acquired the mosaic from the Barberini family.

It's clear that only a relentless passion coupled with exceptional erudition could have assembled such an outstanding collection. Thanks to the generosity and discernment of Giovanni Barrocco, Rome is graced with a superb museum filled with masterpieces from the ancient world.

Museo del Burcardo

The Burcardo Theater Museum

Via del Sudario, N. 44
Rome 00186
Tel: 06/681-9471

Open Monday, Wednesday
and Friday
9:00 A.M. to 1:30 P.M.
Open Tuesday and Thursday
9:00 A.M. to 4:00 P.M.

Bus: 56, 60, 64, 87, 94

THE INTERIOR COURTYARD
OF THE PALAZZO BURCARDO
WAS CONSTRUCTED AT THE END OF
THE SIXTEENTH CENTURY.
THE BURCARDO THEATER MUSEUM
IS CONTIGUOUS WITH
THE TEATRO ARGENTINA,
WHERE ROSSINI PREMIERED
THE BARBER OF SEVILLE
AND LUIGI PIRANDELLO STAGED
MANY OF HIS PLAYS.

Few people today may be aware that Rome's famous Piazza Torre Argentina was named after a picturesque Renaissance edifice built in 1503 for Bishop Hans Burckhardt, author of a remarkable account of the papal court under Innocent VIII and Alexander VI.

Once called the Torre Argentina (because of its tower, long since removed), the building now houses the Burcardo Theater Museum, an edifice which, coincidentally, has a number of significant thespian connections. Not only are its foundations built upon the ruins of Pompey's Roman theater (the first masonry theater in ancient Rome), but its courtyard also abuts the back doors of the Teatro Argentina, Rome's most important theater in the eighteenth century. It was here that, in 1816, Giacomo Rossini presented the debut performance of his *Barber of Seville* and, in 1851, Giuseppe Verdi premiered *Rigoletto*. (The theater is now noted for repertory drama—Teatro di Roma is its resident company.)

As the result of a handsome restoration, visitors can now admire some of the building's original ceiling and pagan frieze decorations, together with fragments from a wall fresco showing a topographical view of Jerusalem and the city's holy places (including the Mosque of Omar).

In choosing to respect the building's historical and cultural context, while showcasing five centuries of theatrical memorabilia, the directors have contributed substantially to this museum's originality and charm. The elegant glass-and-steel display cases and fiber-optic lighting demonstrate that past and present can not only co-exist beautifully, but actually enhance one another.

The core of the theatrical collection was donated by Luigi Rasi, an actor, and later director of the Acting School of Florence, as well as an erudite theatrical historian. After his death in 1918, the entire bequest, which had been offered in vain to the Ministry of Education, was purchased by the Italian Society for the Rights of Authors and Publishers (S.I.A.E.), thanks to the interest of its president, the celebrated actor Marco Praga. (After its move from Milan to Rome in 1926, the Society obtained from the City of Rome the use of the Palazzetto del Burcardo to house the collection.)

Today, through major donations from actors and playwrights, the collection has been enlarged to include stage costumes, prints, paintings and drawings, playbills, puppets and marionettes, as well as autograph scripts and set designs.

Among the most interesting items on display are a series of handmade leather masks, as well as two brightly colored Harlequin costumes, one from the eighteenth century and one worn by Marcello Moretti (1910–1961), in Goldoni's *Servitore di due padroni (Servant to Two Masters)*. These are the quintessential disguises of the Commedia dell'Arte, the most influential development in the history of comedy.

This theatrical art form originated in the Italian urban centers in the early sixteenth century: street performers would don masks with exaggerated comical features to draw attention to themselves and to complement their acrobatic skills. With a mask concealing their identities, the performers could ridicule any aspect of society and its institutions. Ironically, the more trouble these troupes got into with the political and ecclesiastical authorities, the more popular and successful they became.

The most famous character in the Commedia dell'Arte is *Arlecchino*, or Harlequin, who represented both

THE FIRST-FLOOR GALLERY REVEALS
LAYERS OF HISTORY:
THE LATE SIXTEENTH-CENTURY
PAINTED CEILING FRIEZE
AND THE LOW ARCHED DOORWAY
MARRY WELL WITH
THE CONTEMPORARY GLASS-AND-METAL
VITRINES CONTAINING
RARE PRINTS, PHOTOS, AND
MANUSCRIPTS.
NOTE THE COLLECTION OF
EIGHTEENTH-CENTURY CHINESE
MARIONETTES ON STICKS
IN THE GLASS CASE TO THE LEFT.

a numbskull and a clown; he is credited, partly because of his stick, for originating slapstick comedy. Bratty and obtuse, his movements tend to be jerky and defensive, and he's always on the lookout for well-deserved blows.

Originally Arlecchino's costume

consisted of breeches and a long jacket that was laced in front, and covered with random patches in different colors to denote poverty. Not until the seventeenth century did these patches take the form of blue, red, and green triangles arranged in a symmetrical pattern, which the French then transformed into diamonds, a style which has become internationally recognizable.

As traveling performers, the actors in a Commedia dell'Arte troupe went from city to city, transporting all their stage equipment with them, including backdrop, curtains, and stage props. Their carts could be transformed into stage platforms complete with storage and backstage areas. Commonplace among their backdrop designs were

TWO HARLEQUIN COSTUMES:
THE ONE IN THE FOREGROUND DATES BACK TO THE EIGHTEENTH CENTURY;
THE OTHER WAS WORN BY MARCELLO MORETTI
OF THE FAMED PICCOLO TEATRO, DIRECTED BY GIORGIO STREHLER.

perspective views of public squares and streets that their audience could easily recognize. These street entertainers became so much part of public life in Italy and France over the centuries that they inspired countless engravings, paintings, and even puppets.

Among the rarities in the collection are Jacques Callot's (1593–1635) etchings of courtiers, beggars, and hunchbacks based on characters from the Commedia dell'Arte. (Callot, considered one of the greatest and most productive etchers, with 1,500 plates to his credit, is best known for his terrifying record of savagery during the Thirty Years' War.)

While many wealthy Italian nobles, merchants, and churchmen (particularly the Jesuits) took a great interest in the theater, often building private theaters in their palaces and reviving performances of classical Roman plays, traveling theatrical companies were still treated as society's outcasts. Civil authorities were worried that they might be potential carriers of the plague, and might also cause public unrest, should their audiences have too much to drink at a given performance. This is why some towns would go so far as to ban the performance of plays and even refuse a company's entry into town.

Among the museum's exhaustive collection of playbills and theater programs are seventeenth- and eighteenth-century edicts on theater attendance, theatrical bans from the Cisalpine Republic, as well as examples of police regulations pertaining to theaters and dances from the first half of the nineteenth century. Yet even in a society that was prone to bans and regulations, there was also room for adulation of the acting community, judging by

PUPPETEERS NEEDED GREAT STRENGTH
TO LIFT THESE
ARMED SICILIAN MARIONETTES,
WHICH REPRESENT KNIGHTS
FROM THE COURT OF CHARLEMAGNE.

the rare playbills made of silk, and the verses and dedications that paid homage to actors and playwrights.

While the collection highlights the costumes and photographs of such nationally renowned performers as Tatiana Pavlova, Gemma Caimmi, and Ettore Petrolini, the most affecting tribute is to Eleanora Duse (1859–1924), shown in both period photographs and in a fine, full-length portrait by Edoardo Gordigiani (1830–1909). With her portrayal of Alexandre Dumas Fils's *La Dame aux Camélias* in 1893 in New York and London, as well as her role as Magda in Hermann Sudermann's *Heimat*, she became the only true rival to Sarah Bernhardt.

THESE ELABORATE AND ELEGANT
COSTUMES ONCE BELONGED TO
ANNA FOUGEZ (1894–1966),
A CELEBRATED VARIETY SINGER
AND ACTRESS.

Duse's acting was characterized by extreme simplicity and a lack of artifice. She excelled in emotional parts, and her dramatic power, however restrained, was tremendous in its effect. Seeing the photographs of Duse taken when she starred in Ibsen's *Rosmersholm*, it is easy to see why she captured the hearts of so many theater-goers, not to mention that of the Italian poet Gabriele D'Annunzio, whose plays she was often the first to present and champion.

Luigi Pirandello (1867–1936), one of the great figures in twentieth-century European theater, who won the 1934 Nobel Prize for Literature, is grippingly portrayed by Primo Conti (1900–1988). This portrait hangs above one of the museum's most precious possessions: an autographed, annotated script in both Italian and Sicilian dialect of Pirandello's *Liolà*. Although the prolific Pirandello wrote seven novels and nearly three hundred short stories, his fame rests primarily on his bizarre and highly cerebral plays. He began writing for the theater during World War I, and from that point on, produced more than forty dramas, which by 1924 were being performed in most of the world's capitals. Today his best-known plays include *Right You Are When You Think You Are* and *Six Characters In Search of An Author.*

The grim humor of his theater originates from a central theme—the mind-shattering struggle to differentiate between reality and illusion. Pirandello saw reality as an intangible, and that which is taken for reality as often a series of illusions. If truth were not ascertainable, his characters would be condemned to live in moral and cultural chaos. Some critics believe that the playwright's deep-seated alienation contributed to his support of the dictator Benito

Mussolini, because he represented "a man of order."

While the collections at the Burcardo Theater Museum are bound to appeal particularly to the specialist and the devoted theater-goer, its director, Maria Teresa Iovinelli, hopes that they will eventually spur a renewed interest in Italian as well as international, theater. "This museum could play a valuable role for children in school, most of whom still don't go to the theater much," she says.

Meanwhile, visitors to this vibrant museum have an opportunity to explore the fascinating and varied theatrical heritage of Italy, which has indubitably enriched and inspired the world's stage and screen.

Museo della Casina delle Civette

The Museum of the Swiss Cottage of the Owls

Via Nomentana, N. 70
Rome 00161
Tel: 06/442–50072

**Open Tuesday through Sunday
9:00 A.M. to 7:00 P.M.
April 1 to September 30.
9:00 A.M. to 5:00 P.M.
October 1 to March 31.**

**Bus: 36, 36b, 37, 60, 62, 136,
137, 310, 317
Metro: B (Bologna)**

Far from the major Roman monuments, inside a park that was originally designed for Prince Giovanni Torlonia in 1806, visitors will discover one of the most incongruous sites in this city: a charming "gingerbread-style" cottage, notable for its colorful tile-covered gables and roofing, its multiple balconies, as well as its numerous windows and doors in a variety of shapes and sizes.

Originally conceived by the Venetian architect Giuseppe Jappelli in 1840 as a Swiss Cottage, the house was intended to be a bucolic and informal retreat in marked contrast to the nearby Neoclassical Torlonia Villa designed by Louis Valadier (which was, at one time, the home of Benito

THE GINGERBREAD-LIKE SWISS COTTAGE OF THE OWLS IN THE VILLA TORLONIA
IS AN ASTONISHING COMPENDIUM OF ARCHITECTURAL STYLES, MOSAICS, POLY-
CHROME WINDOWS, PAINTED WROUGHT-IRONWORK, AND MARBLE SCULPTURES.

Mussolini). Then in 1908, the young Prince Giovanni Torlonia, a wealthy dandy and aesthete, decided to live in the cottage on a permanent basis, and commissioned the architect Gennari to impart to the cottage a Neo-Gothic appearance by adding a number of tufa towers. The final major metamorphosis was carried out between 1916 and 1920 by the architect Vincente Fasolo (1885–1969), who added the cottage's loggias and ornamental porticoes.

While it may seem difficult to qualify the cottage's overall design, most Romans refer to it as "Liberty" or "*stile* Liberty," a term taken from the English retail shop that Arthur Lasenby Liberty opened in London's Regent Street in 1875. Known as the first "lifestyle" shop specializing in elegant textiles, fashions, and jewelry inspired by Celtic motifs and organic forms, the retailer built up an international reputation designing and printing textiles in exclusive patterns and colors, which were then exported to continental Europe and the United States.

Liberty's fanciful animal and geometric designs and bold floral patterns were flamboyant and daring at the time. Soon, Italian textile firms were inspired to create similar motifs, so that some of the earliest innovations in twentieth-century design were typecast as "Liberty."

Other Italian architects, artists, and designers, also associated the term "Liberty" with "Art Nouveau," an avant-garde movement whose aim was to make a deliberate break with the past, by sweeping away the historicism of the Victorian age, which still found comfort and security in watered-down styles such as Neo-Gothic, Neo-Renaissance and Neo-Baroque. (The term "Art Nouveau" came into widespread usage after the opening of Siegfried Bing's Galerie de

STAINED-GLASS WINDOWS
DEPICTING A GROUP OF BIRDS FLYING
THROUGH THE CLOUDS
ARE AMONG THE PASTORAL FEATURES
IN THE SWISS COTTAGE OF THE OWLS.

L'Art Nouveau in Paris in December 1895.)

Artists were no longer limited to a single art form, but were encouraged to express themselves in a multiplicity of disciplines allowing them to create an entire range of products, from furniture to tapestries, glassware and ceramics, wallpaper and textiles. The most vocal proponents of this new ideology were William Morris, artist, socialist, and bookbinder, and leader of the Arts and Crafts Movement, and Emile Gallé, the French ceramicist and furniture designer from the School of Nancy.

Art Nouveau used free-flowing motifs based on nature, inspired in part by the lessons of Japonisme with its emphasis on sinuous and flowing lines. In describing the essence of this style, art historian Geoffrey Warren writes: "Think of a sensuous line, of

THE COTTAGE'S MOST BEAUTIFUL AND SIGNIFICANT STAINED-GLASS WINDOWS
BY DUILIO CAMBELLOTTI FEATURE A CASCADE OF GRAPES AND VINE LEAVES.

a flowing line, a line which bends and turns back on itself. Think of the feminine form, round and curving. Think of plant forms growing and burgeoning. Think of flowers in bud, in overblown blossoms, as seed pods. Think of waves, think of women's hair, think of twisting smoke."

Art Nouveau also aimed to become a "total art" that would do away with the duality between form and ornamentation, in favor of an overall unity and harmony in design. Prince Torlonia sought to attain this

THIS STAIRWELL'S CEILING FEATURES FOUR STAINED-GLASS RHOMBI OF *THE MIGRANTS*,
ILLUSTRATING FLOCKS OF BIRDS IN PERPETUAL FLIGHT.

ideal at the Casina delle Civette: for instance, the prevalent theme of the owl is reproduced so obsessively both in its architecture and stained-glass windows, that it inspired the cottage's name. In its heyday, the cottage was decorated with mural paintings, mosaic floors, stuccos, majolicas, and numerous stained-glass windows notable for their fantastic and pastoral Art Nouveau imagery.

One must recognize that the present museum is a far cry from the residence Prince Torlonia once occupied. After his death in 1939, the chalet was abandoned; then, between 1944 and 1947, the estate was inhabited by the Anglo-American military command, a period of time during which the already fragile structure suffered sizable damage. When the municipality of Rome purchased Villa Torlonia in 1978, the Casina was in a deplorable state.

Thanks to a thoughtful restoration

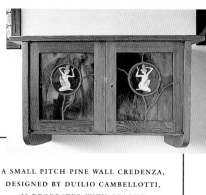

A SMALL PITCH-PINE WALL CREDENZA, DESIGNED BY DUILIO CAMBELLOTTI, IS DECORATED WITH OPAQUE ART NOUVEAU STAINED-GLASS WINDOWS.

process, the chalet's different phases of construction have been respected. Those who tour the house will be able to appreciate all the ways Fasolo used different materials, including brick, tufa stone, and zinc, to create organic forms intended to be in harmony with the surrounding park and gardens.

Still, the principal attraction of the house is its stained-glass windows, decorating doors, armoires, and cabinets, as well as floor-to-ceiling windows and bays. The most beautiful and impressive windows are by Duilio Cambellotti (1876–1960); referred to as the *Chiodo* (the Nail), because of their form, these very large, thin glass windows feature a cascade of vine leaves and bunches of grapes, so real-

istic that one can almost imagine that a grape arbor has been growing indoors. Cambellotti also created the stained-glass windows depicting the owl, the leitmotif of the house.

Paolo Paschetto (1885–1963), who favored making stained-glass windows in a series, contributed the four rhombi of *The Migrants,* illustrating birds in perpetual flight, an apt choice for an overhead skylight in one of the chalet's stairwells. This artist's appreciation of the forces in nature is also evident in his stained-glass window of ascending birds *(The Wings),* as well as in his series of windows depicting the pollination process between the rose and the butterfly.

While Umberto Bottazzi's (1865–1932) dazzling stained-glass windows of *The Peacocks* were never part of the house (they were shown in 1912 in a major Italian exhibition of Art Nouveau stained glass), they were recently purchased and added to the collection.

Inspired by the landscapes, greenery, and flowers which ornamented furniture, textiles, and wallpaper, artists and designers found in stained-glass windows a clear, transparent, and luminous surface. As they experimented with new techniques, they discovered that by superimposing different layers of glass and making them opaque, it seemed as if light was being filtered through an overcast and clouded sky.

With the invention of the incandescent electric light bulb, stained-glass windows were designed to represent an idyllic universe of animals, vegetation, and flowers, a poetic world exalted by poets, that in effect was a refuge from the brutality of the modern Industrial Age. Such was the impulse informing the creations of the stained-glass artists who worked at the Casina delle Civette.

THESE ROSE-AND-BUTTERFLY THEMED STAINED-GLASS WINDOWS
ARE BY PAOLO PASCHETTO.

Stained-glass techniques had changed little since they were first developed in the eleventh century. An artist first made a small-scale sketch of the design, then a cartoon, consisting of a full-size plan drawn with lead or tin point on a wooden board or table coated with chalk or white paint. Pieces of different colored glass were placed together in this full-size drawing of the window, then joined with lead strips, which were soldered into place. The glass panels were then assembled into the window frame. The original water-color designs of stained-glass windows from the period, including of windows at the cottage, help visitors to visualize this process from its earliest stage.

There is a mystery to glass; after all, it is a form of matter that happens to have gas, liquid, and solid state properties. Its ability to capture light and glow from within gives it an energy and dynamism that reinforces the tenets of Art Nouveau. Thanks to the restoration of the Casina delle Civette, there now exists a delight-fully whimsical museum where one can appreciate the beauty and originality of this period's stained-glass windows.

Museo della Ceramica-Palazzo Brugiotti

The Ceramic Museum in the Brugiotti Palace

Via Cavour, N. 67
Viterbo 01100
Tel: 0761/346–136

Open Thursday, Friday, Saturday, and Sunday 10:00 A.M. to 1:00 P.M. and 4:00 P.M. to 8:00 P.M. April through September. Open Tuesday, Saturday, and Sunday 10:00 A.M. to 1:00 P.M. and 3:00 P.M. to 7:00 P.M. October through March.

By bus: Cottral from the Rome Bus Station Saxa-Rubra to Viterbo. Get off at Porta Romano and walk ten minutes until you reach Via Cavour. By car: Cassia Bis highway to Viterbo.

During the period when the plague known as the "Black Death" decimated almost half the population of Europe between 1347 and 1350, the remains of meals, dirtied water, and even ordinary household objects were buried in wells dug out of soft tufa stone, in an effort to reduce the spread of this highly infectious disease. At that time, each house had one or more wells to contain this refuse, which were walled up and covered over with soil once they were full.

Over the past twenty years, during the restoration of the historic centers in Upper Latium, many of these wells

THE PALAZZO BRUGIOTTI,
WHICH HOUSES THE CERAMIC MUSEUM,
IS IN THE HEART OF
VITERBO'S HISTORIC MEDIEVAL
DISTRICT.

THE ENTRANCE TO
THE PALAZZO BRUGIOTTI
IS SET OFF BY
THIS HANDSOME RENAISSANCE
FOUNTAIN.

have been uncovered, revealing a rich hoard of ceramic fragments dating from the Middle Ages. These pieces were gathered together and studied in an effort to reconstitute the history of earthenware production in Upper Latium, an undertaking that has enabled scholars to ascertain that its beginnings can be traced back to the developments of the first towns during the twelfth and thirteenth centuries. It is a tribute to the ingenuity and dedication of local artisans and ceramic experts that these pieces have been so painstakingly reassembled and organized.

These exceptional pieces of simple Italian earthenware and early *majolica* can now be admired in the elegant Ceramic Museum in the heart of Viterbo's historic district. Located on the ground floor of the Palazzo Brugiotti, a fine example of late-Renaissance architecture, the museum's collection of 200 ceramics is displayed in cool and dimly lit rooms which only serve to enhance their luster and mystery.

In light of its history, it seems altogether fitting that Viterbo was selected to house such a collection. As one of the best-preserved walled Medieval towns in all of Italy, it has a lengthy history of producing ceramics. In fact, the town charter of 1251 lists set rules for producing and trading simple pottery.

It was around this time that Italian potters became familiar with the technique for making *majolica,* a type of glazed pottery originally imported from the island of Majorca. This process consists of first firing a piece of earthenware, then applying a tin-based enamel that, upon drying, forms a white opaque porous surface. A design is then painted on this surface and a transparent glaze applied. Finally, the piece is fired again.

THESE PHARMACEUTICAL JARS WITH UNDECIPHERABLE MARKINGS,
FOUND BENEATH THE FOUNDATIONS OF THE OLD HOSPITAL OF VITERBO,
WERE ONCE USED TO HOLD OLIVE OIL AND HERB-SCENTED WATERS,
WHICH WERE THOUGHT TO HAVE RESTORATIVE PROPERTIES.

While this type of ware was produced in the ancient Middle East by the Babylonians, and was extensively used by Hispano-Moresque potters in Spain, it only became popular in Italy during the fourteenth century. Its appeal soon became widespread, and by the mid-fifteenth century *majolica* was being produced in many different areas close to cities where there was a substantial demand for such wares.

The museum's chronological exhibition helps to provide a framework for understanding the usage and development of earthenware production in Southern Italy during the Middle Ages and later. The tour begins with primitive twelfth-century *panate* (bowls for a kind of soup made with dried bread, water, herbs, and olive oil), then moves on to the "green family" of ceramics, then pieces with the characteristic cobalt blue decoration called *zaffera* (sapphire). The exhibition is rounded out with fifteenth-century and seventeenth-century ceramic grocery and pharmaceutical containers, including *albarellos,* which were an early means of measure, along with a stunning collection of decorative presentation plates, which were often given to a prospective bride.

"Among the oldest bowls we found made in Viterbo were for *panata* and for *aqua cotta,* a kind of hot drink made with eggs," explains Dott.ssa Francesca Riccio, the museum's director. "Most of the pieces were doubtless owned by the wealthy or people of means," she adds. "The poor could not have afforded them."

By coating the clay with this pewtered, opaque, and impermeable white enamel *(blanco),* dishes could be more elaborately decorated. The so-called "green family" of ceramics consists of bowls and jugs painted with fantastic animals in a shade of green made from copper oxide, while their brown contours were obtained by using manganese oxide.

The stylized crosses and swastikas on some of the other plates made during this period lead experts to believe that some of these ceramics might have belonged to Crusaders, notably the Knights Templars, a chivalrous order originally founded early in the twelfth century to protect pilgrims on their way to Jerusalem. Given the eventual fate of these crusaders, it is all the more moving to see vestiges of their former wealth.

Recognized at the Council of Troyes in 1128 and confirmed by Pope Honorius III, the Templars received gifts of estates and money and soon became one of the most powerful bodies in Europe during the Middle Ages. By combining monastic privilege with opportunities for chivalrous adventure, they attracted many nobles to their ranks. Although they originally distinguished themselves in fighting Muslims during the Crusades, after the fall of Jerusalem, they ceased fighting, eventually becoming the leading moneylenders of Europe, answerable only to the Pope.

As their wealth and landholdings grew, they aroused the jealousy, fear, and hostility of secular rulers and the clergy. In 1307, Philip IV "the Fair" of France (who needed money for his Flemish war and was unable to obtain it elsewhere), began a persecution of the Templars. With the aid of Pope Clement V, he had members of the order arrested and their possessions confiscated. The knights were then put on trial and tortured to extract confessions of sacrilegious practices. While the Pope first opposed these trials, he soon reversed his position, and at the Council of Vienna dissolved the Order of the Knights

THE MUSEUM'S GALLERY STILL RETAINS THE SIMPLE, SPARE LINES
OF THE PALACE'S EARLY RENAISSANCE ARCHITECTURE,
A FITTING SETTING FOR THESE MEDIEVAL CERAMICS FROM VITERBO.

Templars by papal bull. By 1314, the Templars had been completely destroyed as an organization, and their vast holdings absorbed by Philip IV and his allies.

Viterbo's ceramics reached their apogee during the first half of the fifteenth century, with the development of a *majolica* known as *zaffèra*—white-glazed pottery decorated with deep sapphire blue bas-reliefs of vines, animals, and mythological creatures, half-man,

half-beast, made with a cobalt-blue oxide. "This oxide was made with lapis lazuli, which had to be imported from the Orient or from Egypt," notes Dott.ssa Riccio. "It was very rare and very costly—in fact, worth as much as gold."

While Viterbo's production of ceramics declined during the second half of the fifteenth century, other majolica centers, such as those in Faenza, Gubbio, Deruta, Urbino, and Castro, flourished. Thanks to the

SHARDS OF POTTERY FRAME THIS PLATE
DECORATED WITH A SOLAR ECLIPSE,
MADE IN VITERBO IN 1431.

existence of Cipriano Piccolpasso's *The Three Books of the Potter's Art* (c. 1555), scholars are now able to establish the different techniques and types of decorations that were used.

It appears that around 1500 or so, a major innovation in pottery took hold in Faenza—the use of engravings or paintings, which gave birth to the decor of *istoriato* or histories. This entailed illustrating plates with different pagan myths or stories from the Bible, an innovation that would later be adopted in Urbino and culminate in a period of rich and abundant production. Often these stylized drawings were used to decorate *piatti di pompa* (presentation plates).

Wealthy families commissioned *istoriato* that would be decorated with their name and coat-of-arms. One plate in the museum pays tribute to the powerful Colonna family, depicting Aphrodite, the goddess of beauty, next to a column, the symbol for the family's coat-of-arms.

In imitation of Hispano-Moresque pieces, the town of Deruta developed a special technique of additional firing to impart a metallic sheen to ceramic objects. One of the finest ornamental plates from Deruta, decorated with a lion under a palm tree (the seal of Isabella of Aragon), and made in the first half of the sixteenth century, illustrates this technique. (This is the same Isabella who married Ferdinand of Aragon, established the Inquisition under royal control, was a prime mover in the expulsion of the Jews and the Moors from Spain in 1492, and showed remarkable foresight in her patronage of Christopher Columbus.)

Yet perhaps the most alluring ceramics in this intriguing collection are the plates given to prospective brides, which portray elegant Renaissance women in elaborate headdress and brocades, set off by an abbreviated inscription extolling their charms, such as *Simone est b.* (meaning "Simone is beautiful"). The ground of the plate was usually painted dark blue, which helped to set off the face, and the young woman's expression.

As these lovely painted faces gaze back at the visitor, one can only contemplate admiringly the ingenuity of scores of Italian artisans, who were able to create such lasting works of beauty and artistry with such simple materials and means as clay, paint, glazes, and fire.

DECORATED WITH FANTASTIC ANIMALS
AND VEGETAL FORMS IN GREEN AND BROWN GLAZES,
THESE EARTHENWARE PIECES
ARE TYPICAL OF THOSE MADE IN THE
FIRST HALF OF THE FIFTEENTH CENTURY IN UPPER LAZIO.

THIS PLATE, A WEDDING GIFT,
WHICH IS DECORATED
WITH THE ARMS OF ISABELLA OF ARAGON,
WAS MADE IN DERUTA IN
THE FIRST HALF OF THE SIXTEENTH CENTURY.

Museo Criminologico di Roma

The Rome Museum of Criminology

Via Del Gonfalone, N. 29
Rome 00186
Tel: 06/6830–0234

Open Tuesday 9:00 A.M. to
1:00 P.M. and 2:30 P.M. to
6:30 P.M.
Open Thursday from 2:30 P.M.
to 6:30 P.M.
Open Wednesday, Friday, and
Saturday 9:00 A.M. to 1:00 P.M.
Closed Sunday, Monday,
holidays, and in August.

Bus: 64, 116, 280

S TROLLING down the fashionable Via Giulia with its elegant
Baroque villas and lines of expensive
cars, it comes as a surprise to find the
Rome Museum of Criminology,
which is housed in a building that was
once used as a prison. Built for Pope
Leo XII in 1827 and designed by
the French architect Louis Valadier
(who also created the Piazza del
Populo), this former prison site also
happens to contain offices for the
city's Police Department.

After undergoing a security check
and entering through a double (likely
bulletproof) revolving glass door,
even the most blameless visitor might
understandably feel a twinge of

THE EDIFICE HOUSING THE ROME MUSEUM OF CRIMINOLOGY
IS PART OF A FORMER PRISON
BUILT BY LOUIS VALADIER BETWEEN 1825 AND 1827.
VALADIER ALSO DESIGNED THE PIAZZA DEL POPULO AFTER
NAPOLEON BONAPARTE'S CONQUEST OF ITALY.

apprehension. This sensation is further heightened upon catching sight of the corroded Mantellate bronze bell, celebrated in Roman songs and ballads, which once marked time during the tedious daily routine to which prisoners were subjected.

This atypical museum, whose exhibits range from Medieval torture instruments to forensic evidence to a gallery of forged antiquities and works of art, provides an encyclopedic overview of the evolution of crime and punishment since the days of ancient Rome. Divided into three chronological sections, the museum devotes one exhibit area to "The Social Control of Deviance," to examine the subject of penitentiary evolution and the recent history of prisons in Italy, and dedicates another to "The Spirit of Reason," which focuses on the development of criminal anthropology and techniques for reconstructing crimes. Yet it is the section dubbed "Punishment and Crimes," demonstrating how criminals were dealt with in the past, that turns out to be the most chilling and the most morbidly fascinating.

Using miniature and life-size prototypes, (some of which were made by juvenile offenders), as well as antique illustrations and engravings, this exhibition illustrates various methods of punishment that have been used for centuries throughout Europe, and shows how instruments of torture demonstrated a ruler's power. "The tortured body of the victim was an expression of the obsession with punishment that typified the Dark Ages," writes Dott.ssa Assunta Borzacchiello, in the museum's catalogue. "It was a time when the lack of legal certainties meant that limitless forms of punishment and pain could be inflicted."

This seems an understatement when looking at a reconstruction of

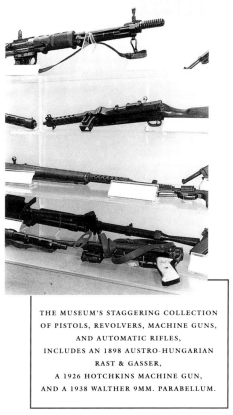

THE MUSEUM'S STAGGERING COLLECTION OF PISTOLS, REVOLVERS, MACHINE GUNS, AND AUTOMATIC RIFLES, INCLUDES AN 1898 AUSTRO-HUNGARIAN RAST & GASSER, A 1926 HOTCHKINS MACHINE GUN, AND A 1938 WALTHER 9MM. PARABELLUM.

the Iron Maiden, an instrument of death that belonged to the court of Nuremberg in Germany. This iron anthropomorphic container had spikes pointing inward, so that when a person was placed inside and the two doors of the unit were closed, the spikes penetrated the victim's flesh.

Another horrific instrument of torture was known as the "mute's bridle," a heavy iron mask from the Middle Ages that was used to stifle a victim's screams so as not to disturb the interrogators' conversation. The iron "tongue" on the inside of the bridle ring was forced into the victim's mouth while the iron collar was fastened behind the neck. A small hole allowed the passage of air, but this could be stopped by a touch of the executioner's fingertip, which would then induce suffocation. Often

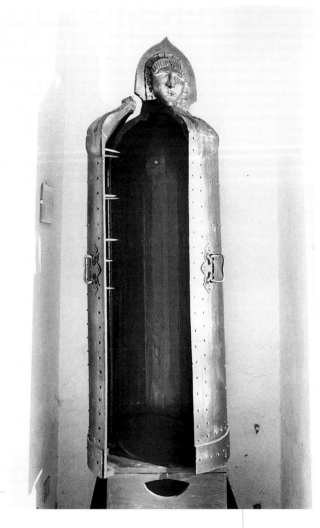

THIS IS A COPY OF THE VIRGIN OF NUREMBERG—AN INSTRUMENT OF TORTURE THAT WAS EMPLOYED DURING THE INQUISITION.

those condemned to the stake were thus gagged, especially during the *autos-da-fé* ("acts of faith")— grandiose public festivities in which dozens of heretics were burnt at one time. It seems that their screams would have interfered with the sacred music!

Giordano Bruno (1548–1600), a Renaissance humanist and an early proponent of cosmic theory (which states that the physical world is composed of irreducible elements in constant motion and that the universe is infinite in scope), was condemned by the Inquisition to burn at the stake in the Piazza del Campo dei Fiori in Rome (where his statue stands today). To heighten his punishment, the executioners inserted an iron gag with two spikes into Bruno's mouth, one of which pierced his tongue, the other his palate. No doubt, the ultimate deterrent to free speech!

To extract confessions from religious heretics, the Church authorities

THE GUILLOTINE SERVED AS
AN INSTRUMENT OF EXECUTION IN ROME
UNTIL 1870.
NEXT TO IT IS THE IRON "CAGE OF MILAZZO,"
IN WHICH A HUMAN SKELETON WAS FOUND
AROUND 1928.
THE SMALLER GUILLOTINE ON THE LEFT
WAS ONCE USED TO CUT OFF A PERSON'S HANDS.

would also resort to using torture chairs with spiked seats, forcing the victim to sit on the chair while it was being rocked, so that the nails would lacerate his body. Hard-core apostates were subjected to an instrument of torture aptly titled the "crib of Judas." A scale model shows that the suspect would be seated on the summit of a pyramidal structure while heavy stones, attached to both his arms and legs, pulled his limbs downward. It is not difficult to see how anyone might have confessed to almost anything, given this sort of inducement.

This museum also highlights the repressive ferocity of certain ecclesiastical authorities against women, as well as its often fatal consequences. Witch-hunts were commonplace and rampant; recent scholarship has revealed that between 1450 and 1800, as many as four million European women were condemned as witches in both Catholic and Protestant Europe, and were victims of torture and death at the stake.

A display of "scold's bridles," also known as "branks," shows how women who were viewed as either outspoken or malicious were forced

AMONG THE CHILLING EXHIBITS ON DISPLAY
ARE THE RED CAPE AND BLOOD-STAINED AXE THAT BELONGED TO
ROME'S FAMOUS EXECUTIONER, "MASTRO TITTA."
THE BLOOD-ENCRUSTED GLOVES WERE WORN BY THE HANGMAN OF ALEXANDRIA,
WHILE THE HEMP NOOSE WAS USED TO HANG MURDERERS.

to wear iron contraptions that permanently mutilated their tongues. Singled out by the crowd, they were often publicly humiliated.

While most visitors might assume that these instruments of death, torture, and mortification were used mainly during the Middle Ages, the museum shows that many continued to be popular until the nineteenth century. One of the most terrifying examples is the "cage of Milazzo" named after the town in Sicily where it was found in 1928 by prisoners who were digging outside the local prison. Inside the cage was the skeleton of an English soldier who had fought against the French in the battle of Maida. It seems that the soldier had deserted, then been captured, sentenced to death, and had his body exposed in a cage as an example. This gruesome incident took place in 1806.

While it's easy to deplore the barbaric methods of punishment of the past, the museum also demon-strates (in the section covering criminal anthropology), that many of the issues surrounding crime and punishment remain unresolved to this day. An exhibition on Cesare Lombroso (1836–1909), regarded as the father of criminal anthropology, shows that he believed that by exam-ining the bodies of dead criminals he could uncover the physical anomalies that were linked to the constitutional origin of their crimes.

Lombroso was convinced his theory had been vindicated after the autopsy of the seventy-year-old Calabrian brigand Giuseppe Vilella revealed that there was a pit or depression in his skull. In 1906, this discovery seemed the final piece of evidence Lombroso needed to substantiate his theory of the "constitutional or atavistic criminal." Among the items on display in this section are the cast of Vilella's skull.

Meanwhile, other social scientists were challenging Lombroso's theory, noting that social factors, including poverty and violence, could also contribute to a life of crime. While Lombroso first asserted that seventy percent of criminal behavior was atavistic, by the end of his life he had lowered this figure to thirty-five percent. Nonetheless, the theory of the congenital criminal remained constant in Lombroso's thinking— a theory that challenges the validity of certain programs of prison reform and rehabilitation that have become increasingly prevalent.

An extensive section devoted to both strange and lurid crimes—as well as a series of displays illustrating criminal handiwork—ranging from art forgeries, counterfeit money and stamps, to burglary, espionage, organized crime and state terrorism (including that of the infamous Italian Red Brigades who were responsible for kidnapping and assassinating the Italian Prime Minister Aldo Moro in 1978)—amply demonstrates that the annals of crime have yet to be exhausted.

It is with great relief that visitors discover at the end of this exhaustive and somewhat draining itinerary a room that has been left completely empty—in this instance, an eloquent and hopeful statement about the future of malfeasance. While crime has proven harder to eradicate than most infectious diseases, this unusual museum enables visitors to better comprehend how society's notions of crime and condemnation have evolved over the centuries. And with its plethora of instruments of torture and punishment, one can see how ingeniously and with what determina-tion governing authorities have striven down through the ages to ensure that "Crime doesn't pay."

Museo Donazione Umberto Mastroianni

The Umberto Mastroianni Museum

Piazza San Salvatore in
Lauro, N. 15
Rome 00186
Tel: 06/687-8737

Open from 10:00 A.M.
to 1:00 P.M. daily.
Visits only by pre-arranged
appointment.

Bus: 64, 116, 280

INSIDE THE CLOISTER'S COURTYARD
MASTROIANNI'S FORCEFUL AND ENER-
GETIC SCULPTURES PROVIDE A STRIK-
ING CONTRAST TO THE DELICATE
FRIEZES OVER THE DOORWAY.

ROMAN topographers believe that the Church S. Salvatore in Lauro and its piazza were named after the bay or laurel trees that grew there during the Roman era. This lovely church, which has been rebuilt twice, has a Neoclassical façade with a bas-relief depicting the miraculous flight of the sacred house of Loreto. (According to legend, the Holy House of the Virgin in Nazareth was brought to Loreto through the air by angels in 1294.) S. Salvatore in Lauro is now the Church of the Marche, the province in central Italy where Loreto is located.

The hidden jewel of S. Salvatore in Lauro is its cloister, which is entered by a small door to the left of the church. It is one of the most inviting places in Rome, perhaps because of its atmosphere of intimacy and absolute simplicity, a welcome contrast in a city famous for its pomp and grandeur. The cloister was built during the second half of the fifteenth century by Cardinal Latino Orsini, who left his famous library of manuscripts to the Church canons. Unfortunately, like the church itself, this splendid library was burned during the 1527 Sack of Rome.

A rare and beautiful fifteenth-century door decorated with sculptured flowers and children's heads leads from the cloister into a small garden court with a Renaissance fountain, benevolently presided over by a bust of Cardinal Orsini. Upon request, the cloister's custodian will take visitors into the refectory, where they can see both Isaia di Pisa's marble monument to the Venetian Pope Eugene IV (1431–47), brought here from St. Peter's, and Francesco Salviati's beautifully restored fresco depicting the *Wedding Feast at Cana*, at which Jesus turned water into wine.

In *Lives of the Artists*, Giorgio Vasari describes this fresco at length, and also cites a painting (now lost) over the refectory's door of St. George killing the dragon, praising it as "a work executed with great skill, polish, and charm of coloring." Vasari and Salviati were boyhood friends and it is with great pride that the Renaissance chronicler recalls their early exploit in salvaging the broken pieces of Michelangelo's *David*, after its left arm was smashed in a fracas. (The story is evidently true since the breaks are clearly visible in the left arm below the wrist.)

The calm and serenity of this cloister, coupled with its unique artistic heritage, make it an appropriate setting in which to contemplate the work of one of Italy's most inventive, exuberant, and energetic artists, Umberto Mastroianni (1910–1978). Born into a family of artists in Latium's Fontana Liri, his vocation was encouraged at an early age by his uncle Domenico, who invited him to work at his studio in Rome and take drawing lessons at San Marcello's Academy. Two years later he settled in Turin with his family, and pursued his artistic studies in the studio of Michele Guerrieri. When he was only eighteen, he revealed his mastery over the human figure and his ability to create a harmonious and moving composition, as in his bas-relief of the *Deposition* (1928), which represents the silent dialogue between the Virgin and Christ.

Inspired by Egyptian, ancient Greek, and Etruscan sculpture, Mastroianni in his early years dedicated himself to sculpting bronze portrait busts and full-length figures,

wherein he sought to attain the essence of the human figure through streamlining and simplification. At the same time, he drew inspiration from fragmented ancient sculptures he had come to love, creating his own armless and headless works, in which the central energy seems to emanate from the body itself. This is particularly noticeable in his reclining, armless *Nude of Young Athlete* (1938), where all the body's tension seems to reside in the straining torso and uplifted, crossed legs, as well as in the headless *Female Nude* (1939), which appears to be bursting from the bonds of its bronze cast.

THIS BUST OF CARDINAL LATINO ORSINI PRESIDES BENIGNLY OVER THE CLOISTERAL COMPLEX.

During this same period Mastroianni explored figurative portraiture, in gesso, terra-cotta, and bronze, sometimes choosing to simplify facial features to distill a subject's thoughtfulness and serenity, as in *Portrait of a Gentlewoman*

THE BAS-RELIEFS ABOVE THE CLOISTER'S DOORWAY AND ON THE WALLS
DATE BACK TO THE FIFTEENTH CENTURY.

A PANORAMIC OVERVIEW OF MASTROIANNI'S WORKS: IN THE CENTRAL FOREGROUND, *VIOLENCE* (1956); IN THE RIGHT FOREGROUND, *FORCE OF MATTER*, IN WOOD (1970); ON THE REAR WALL, THE CANVAS, *ATUM AND GHEB* (1988).

(1939), at other times showing with great sensitivity an individual's inner self-questioning and pain, as in *Adolescent Bust* (1935).

While these early figurative works were modeled along classical lines, they all contain an inner tension which would soon be released in powerful, pointed, and aggressive sculptures that establish a dynamic, even electric relationship between the viewer and the surrounding environment.

To express this untrammeled energy and movement, Mastroianni was compelled to explore a number of different mediums and techniques, all of which are represented in the collection. Among his most striking works are the colored, scraped, and lacerated abstract paintings on cardboard and wood, such as his brilliantly painted 1952–54 *Night Story,* and his eruptive 1954 *Roots,* as well as his 1958–59 explosive polychromatic relief on cardboard, aptly titled *Organic Essence.* In all these works one can see the raw texture of paint, and the way the artist has manipulated it to depict a world that exudes intense energy and velocity.

The artist continued to explore this theme in the Sixties and Seventies, sometimes using vivid primary colors and industrial materials to express his ideas, as in his 1967 *Firebird,* a relief made of laser-sharp steel and bronze shapes that have been soldered together, then colored with vivid pieces of blue, yellow, orange, and red plastic. By 1972, Mastroianni's reliefs had evolved into dynamic, colored-steel sculptures of soldered circles and triangles, which are best exemplified by such works as *Satellite.*

THESE EARLY FIGURATIVE WORKS IN BRONZE AND TERRA-COTTA
SHOW GREEK AND ETRUSCAN INFLUENCES ON MASTROIANNI'S ART
DURING THE LATE TWENTIES AND EARLY THIRTIES.

Many of these sculptures and bas-reliefs celebrate the Space Age, and humanity's fascination with astronomy and celestial properties: among the artist's finest works on this theme are the white marble *Comet,* which is surprisingly dynamic and thrusting, conveying the immense, unbridled energy of this phenomenon in space, and a wood-and-steel composition of intersecting planes and on-rushing spheres and circles and triangles, aptly titled *Energy Into Space* (both made in 1973).

Such aesthetic choices have compelled art critics to see Mastroianni as the natural successor of the Italian Futurist painter and sculptor Umberto Boccioni (1882–1916), who was persuaded that artists had to burn all bridges with the past, and surrender themselves to the sensations of modern technology. Boccioni's aim was to seize hold of modern life with all its dynamism, vitality, and speed, so that even stationary objects had to be conceived in dynamic terms, broken down into lines of force that conveyed movement, and various stages of a single kinetic sequence. Boccioni's system of perspective involved both simultaneous vanishing points and the abstract representation of objects based on their kinetic properties, an approach that obviously was not lost upon Mastroianni.

Yet, to reduce this artist to being simply a disciple of Boccioni, would be both unfair and inexact. The museum's collection shows that this highly versatile talent was not just taken by the electric energy of the modern age, but was also opposed to the way this new power could be employed for mass destruction and war. A member of the Italian Resistance movement during World War II, Mastroianni gave form to his anti-Fascist and anti-war sentiments in two major works, *Monument to the Resistance at Cuneo* (1964–69) and *Monument to the Dead of All Wars at Frosinone* (1977).

Six haunting China-ink drawings of skeletal figures and skulls *(The*

Resistance), illustrating the horror and terror of war, executed in 1944–45, convey the ravaging devastation that the Allied and Soviet armies were in the midst of discovering in the Nazi concentration camps. A 1957 bronze, *Mask*, of a terrifying and brutal face executed in a series of jagged, Cubist planes, is an unforgettable synthesis of humanity's potential ferocity and alienation. The 1962 *Tragic Sculpture* of twisted, jagged, and melted bronze captures the inexpressible agony and pain that results from untrammeled violence and warfare.

While Mastroianni was compelled to express his outrage against barbarism, his most lasting works are those which celebrate reality's unity, geometry, and energy, demonstrating that its eternal forms are more powerful than any transient horror. This is especially true of his 1970 black marble *Sea-horse* or *Hippogriff,* his 1971 steel *Development of Forms,* and his 1975 *Transmission of*

THIS MONUMENT TO
THE VENETIAN POPE EUGENE IV (1431–47)
WAS SCULPTED BY ISAIA DI PISA IN 1455
AND BROUGHT HERE FROM ST. PETER'S.

Energy. Here the forces of release and containment, thrust and retreat, have been masterfully rearranged and unified by the artist, creating a sense of satisfaction and wonder.

The importance and originality of Mastroianni, were appreciated early on by the noted French art critic Léon Delgard, after the artist's first show in Paris. "What strikes us at once about Mastroianni's art is its perfect harmony with what is lived, organic, and indissoluble, between the figure's proportions and expression, and the discipline and necessities of creation. This unity is so deeply felt by the artist that it succeeds in showing itself with a clarity that is indeed rare." Thanks to this atypical museum in the heart of Rome, visitors can find repose in a serene and quiet cloister while discovering the impressive, thought-provoking works of one of Italy's most innovative artists.

VIBRANT EXPLOSIONS OF COLOR
IN DIFFERENT MEDIA:
THE SCULPTURE OF THE *GYPSY*
IN COLORED WOOD AND SILVER (1987–88);
ON THE REAR WALL, THE TAPESTRY
OF *THE WONDERFUL BIRD* (1989).

Museo Ebraico di Roma

The Jewish Museum of Rome

Lungotevere di Cenci, N. 15
(Tempio)
Rome 00186
Tel: 06/687–5051

**Open Monday through Thursday
9:30 A.M. to 2:00 P.M. and
3:00 P.M. to 7:00 P.M.
Open Friday
9:30 A.M. to 2:00 P.M.
Open Sunday
9:30 A.M. to 12:30 P.M.
Closed Sunday and religious
holidays.
Visits only by pre-arranged
guided tours.**

Bus: 95, 119

THE JEWISH MUSEUM OF ROME IS LOCATED
IN THE SAME BUILDING AS THE SYNAGOGUE,
WHICH WAS INAUGURATED IN 1904.
THE SYNAGOGUE STILL OBSERVES
THE *MINHAG ROMI*
(THE ITALIAN LITURGY OF ROME),
WHICH IS THE OLDEST EUROPEAN LITURGY,
BROUGHT DIRECTLY FROM PALESTINE.

CONVINCED that it was "absurd" for Jews to see themselves the equals of Catholics, on July 14, 1555, Pope Paul IV published his infamous edict *Cum nimis absurdum* establishing the Jewish Ghetto of Rome. Overnight, the Jews of Rome (the most ancient Jewish community in Europe, having arrived in 161 B.C. with Judah Maccabee), were forced to move into the unhealthiest quarter of the city, one that was regularly flooded by the Tiber.

Henceforth, they were allowed to leave the Ghetto only during the day, were forced to wear distinctive headgear, and were permitted to practice only two professions—either selling old clothes and rags or lending money at a fixed rate. Such was their degradation that, during a Roman

carnival, one contemporary observer noted that "they were the only bipeds participating in races in the company of animals," subject to the crowd's violent abuse and mockery.

More than three centuries would pass (until the unification of Italy in 1870 and the annexation of the Papal States by Victor Emmanuel II), before the Jews of Rome would be able to obtain their full civil rights under the law. They would have to wait another sixteen years for the Ghetto's destruction. Yet, only after

THREE *SEFER TORAHS* (SCROLLS OF THE LAW)
DECORATED WITH FINIAL CROWNS AND COVERS.
THE ONE IN THE CENTER, WHICH BELONGED TO THE CATALAN SCHOOL,
HAS A SEVENTEENTH-CENTURY TORAH COVER,
AND IS DECORATED WITH FINIALS MADE BY THE EIGHTEENTH-CENTURY
ROMAN GOLDSMITH GIUSEPPE BARTOLOTTI.

THE MUSEUM'S GROUND-FLOOR GALLERY IS DEDICATED
TO AN EXCEPTIONAL COLLECTION OF ANTIQUE TORAH CURTAINS *(PAROKHETS)*
AND SCROLL COVERS *(MEILS)*,
AS WELL AS ELABORATE DECORATIVE SILVER FINIALS *(RIMMONIM)*,
THAT DECORATE THE TOPS OF THE COVERED TORAHS.

the erection and inauguration in 1904 of a monumental white stone synagogue in the heart of the old Jewish quarter along the Tiber—a synagogue whose imposing cupola was as visible as the basilica of St. Peter's—did Rome's Jews sense that they might consider themselves to be on an equal footing with other Italians.

It is in this very building that the Jewish Museum of Rome was inaugurated in 1967 to illustrate the historical and liturgical heritage of this resilient community, which at the height of the Roman Empire represented ten percent of the city's one million population. The most direct evidence of the organization and administration of ancient Roman Jewry comes from inscriptions in six catacombs used by Jews from the first century to the fourth century A.D.

While some were decorated with frescoes using Hebrew symbols such as the *menorah* (a seven-branched candelabra), others contain mythological symbols, revealing the influence of the pagan world. The language used in the funereal inscriptions on tombstones was almost always Greek and Latin, showing that the Jews in Rome were bilingual.

The belief that there was a numerous and flourishing community in Ostia, at one time the port of Rome, is substantiated by the unearthing of an 850-square-meter synagogue. So far it is the largest and oldest to have been discovered in Europe. It was originally adorned with pillars and mosaics, and contained, in addition to a prayer hall, other rooms for study and for baking unleavened bread, as well as a ritual bath for washing.

Casts of tombstones taken from the ancient Jewish cemetery at Ostia, along with copies of sixteenth-century edicts banning Jews from certain professions, a copy of identity papers stamped with the word "Jew" illustrating the Fascist Racial Laws of 1938, and heartrending photographs of the 1943 Nazi-Fascist raid on the Roman ghetto, during which 2,091 Jews were deported to Auschwitz and Bergen-Belsen concentration camps, are among the museum's exhibits illustrating this community's checkered history in Rome.

Precious silver and vermeil ceremonial objects, jugs and hand-washing basins, and bookbindings, illuminated parchment scrolls with the Book of Esther, as well as ornaments for the Torah scrolls, demonstrate how over the centuries Rome's Jews gloried in their faith despite the heavy restrictions placed upon them and the assiduous attempts made by the Church to convert them. (Starting in 1577, the Jews of Rome were forced to attend Catholic services, preferably officiated by a converted rabbi. This ruling remained in effect until 1870, eliciting all the while protests from Jewish co-religionists, many of whom would yawn, talk, or stop up their ears during the Christian service.)

Rare sixteenth-to-eighteenth-century Roman, Florentine, and Venetian textiles, including velvet, satin, and brocade covers for the Torah scrolls and tablecloths for the pulpit from which the officiant read the Bible and prayers, show that no expense was spared in celebrating the Jewish faith. (Many of these precious cloths were preserved by being hidden inside the ceiling of a Jewish ritual bath or *mikva*, during World War II.) Most of these objects come from the five former Ghetto synagogues, "Cinque Scole," and bear the names of the donor families and the occasions upon which they were given. (Three of the schools were Sephardic—the Catalan School, the Castilian School, and the Sicilian School emigrated to Rome after the Jews' expulsion from Spain in 1492— and the other two were Italian, the

TRADITIONALLY GIVEN TO BRIDES,
THESE PRECIOUS SILVER-COVERED PRAYER BOOKS WERE MADE BETWEEN 1500 AND 1700.

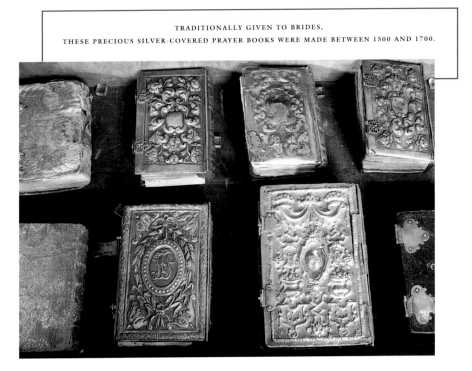

New School and the Temple School.)

"The very concept of a Jewish Museum has seemed an absurdity to certain Jews," observes the museum's director, Anna Ascarelli Bleyer, whose family can be traced back to the expulsion of the Jews from Spain in 1492. "According to the religious laws, liturgical books and objects no longer in use should be annihilated, respectfully buried as God's creatures.

"For this reason, a Jewish museum, such as this one in Rome, is a very special type of museum, first of all because it is a living museum. It's true that these vestments and vessels are shown to the public, but the same objects are also used periodically in ceremonies at the synagogue. Their exhibition is intended to honor the generations preceding us, which—in very difficult times—dedicated so much work and wealth to 'adorn God through the precepts,' according to the teaching of the Talmud.

"The aim of this museum is to both teach and maintain our heritage. Its whole design was especially studied to ensure the best preservation of this large 'living wardrobe' of the Jewish faith."

Contrary to most other religions, which encouraged figurative arts to accompany their forms of worship (be it Roman paganism with its temple and statuary of gods and goddesses, or Catholicism with its basilica decorated with statues, painted altars, and elaborate stained-glass windows), Jewish monotheism placed rigorous limitations and prohibitions on these activities. Any profane image could represent a temptation for the congregation, since a visual representation of the sacred risked humanizing God, by definition invisible and unportrayable.

However, this did not mean that "beautiful objects" could not be used for noble purposes: in the treatise on the Sabbath in the Babylonian Talmud (the rabbinical commentary on Jewish oral law or *halakhah*, the rabbis taught: "Adorn thyself before him in the fulfillment of the precepts. Make . . . a beautiful shofar (the ram's horn which is blown on many solemn occasions), beautiful fringes, and a beautiful Scroll of the Law, and write it with a fine ink, a fine reed-pen, with a skilled penman, and wrap it about with beautiful silks."

The ritual objects from the Renaissance, Baroque, as well as early nineteenth-century periods, reveal to what lengths even impoverished Jews would make sacrifices to commission beautiful objects for their ritual services. The elaborate craftsmanship in ritual washing basins, *menorah* lamps, and embossed silver prayer-book bindings, also reveals the widespread influence of Baroque and Neoclassical motifs. "There may have been a Ghetto in Rome, but there was no artistic ghetto as such," notes Bleyer.

Among the museum's rarities are silver-and-gold-embroidered *parokhets* (Torah ark curtains) and *meils* (Sefer Torah covers), which both protected and beautified the parchment or leather scrolls inscribed with the first five books of the Hebrew Bible, otherwise known as the *Pentateuch*.

When the Torah is not in use, it is encased in the *meil*, and is topped with elaborately decorated gilt or silver finials *(rimmonim)* and crowns *(attarah)*. Among the most intricate finials are those which were made in the seventeenth century, using such varied symbols as the pomegranate, the lion, the crown, and vases of flowers as decoration. These *rimmonim* often were also decked out with tiny bells *(tappuhim)*, to alert the congregation to the oncoming procession of rabbis carrying the Torah.

Each image chosen to decorate the

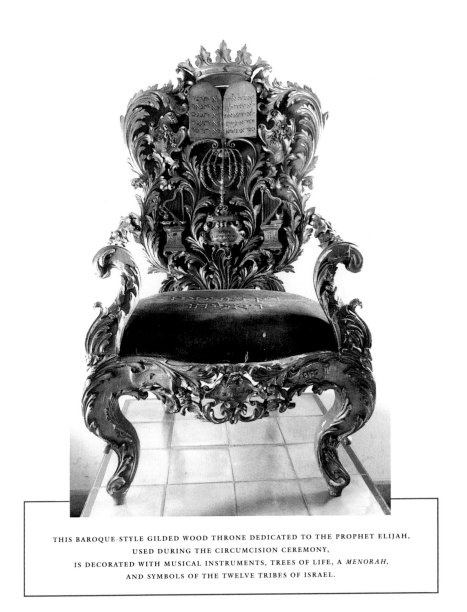

THIS BAROQUE-STYLE GILDED WOOD THRONE DEDICATED TO THE PROPHET ELIJAH,
USED DURING THE CIRCUMCISION CEREMONY,
IS DECORATED WITH MUSICAL INSTRUMENTS, TREES OF LIFE, A *MENORAH*,
AND SYMBOLS OF THE TWELVE TRIBES OF ISRAEL.

finials had a specific meaning intended to glorify some aspect of Judaism. Lions were chosen to symbolize majesty, while the flowerpot motif reflected the traditional Jewish iconography associating the Torah with the Tree of Life. The frequent superposition of crowns *(attarah)* atop the brocade-covered rolled-up Torah scroll illustrated the rabbinical quotation: "There are three crowns, the crown of the Torah, the crown of priesthood and the crown of royalty;

but the crown of a good reputation surpasses them all."

In 1986, when Pope John Paul II visited the synagogue and its museum, he told the congregation, "You are our closest brothers, and even our older brothers." In his statement, he confirmed the implicit message of the Jewish Museum of Rome: that after centuries of suffering and humiliation, there is renewed pride and hope among the Eternal City's Jews.

INGE SCHABEL,
WHOM MANZU MET IN SALZBURG IN 1954,
FIGURES IN NUMEROUS PORTRAITS,
INCLUDING THE LARGE EBONY SCULPTURE
GUANTANAMERA (1968)
WHERE SHE IS REPRESENTED
SITTING WITH ABANDON IN A LARGE ARMCHAIR.

Museo Giacomo Manzù-Ardea

The Giacomo Manzù Museum-Ardea

Via Laurentina Km 32,8
Rome (Ardea) 00040
Tel: 06/9135–022

**Open Tuesday through Sunday
9:00 A.M. to 7:00 P.M.
Open Monday
2:00 P.M. to 7:00 P.M.**

**By bus: Take the Cottral bus
to Ardea from Piazzale G.
Marconi (EUR).
By car: From Via Pontina,
take ss148 to the exit for Ardea,
then follow the signs on Via
Laurentina.**

VISITORS to the Manzù Collection in Ardea will be struck by the originality of Giacomo Manzù (1901–1991), a major post-war Italian sculptor who preferred to master and explore traditional techniques in drawing and sculpture, while maintaining an almost complete indifference to the aesthetic upheaval caused by abstraction.

Commenting on the significance of Manzù's artistic choices, noted art historian and critic John Rewald wrote admiringly: "Giacomo Manzù, in his isolation, kept the classical traditions alive. Obeying an inner necessity, he avoided participating in the experiments of his contemporaries and letting himself be led astray by the charms of the unusual. Instead, he preferred to follow his own feelings and observations, which was more difficult than it may seem."

"Just as Rodin was once accused of having cast one of his male figures directly from the model, so Manzù is accused in some circles of keeping too close to nature. One could say that it almost requires more courage nowadays to remain faithful to nature than to turn one's back on her and pursue the abstract."

Although Manzù's sculptures are now in museums and institutions all over the world, including the Vatican and the United Nations, those who wish to fully appreciate the power of

ON THE RIGHT, TWO PORTRAITS OF INGE SCHABEL IN BRONZE (1967);
IN THE BACKGROUND, *LITTLE GIRL ON THE CHAIR* (1955);
AND ON THE WALL, AN OIL OF *THE ARTIST WITH HIS MODEL.*

his main body of work must journey to an elegant, contemporary museum in Ardea, which has been open since 1969. Representing the artist's mature period between 1950 and 1970, the collection includes 462 sculptures, drawings, engravings, jewels, and medals.

Born to poor parents in Bergamo, Manzù had to leave school at the age of eleven in order to find a job and help support his family. Because of his unusual manual dexterity, he was apprenticed first to a carpenter, and later to a wood-carver. When he turned thirteen he went to work for a gilder, and after that, a stucco-worker. Those years of apprenticeship provided a series of splendid opportunities for the young boy to become thoroughly familiar with various artistic techniques, which would stand him in good stead, since he could not afford formal artistic training (aside from a few classes in sculpture at the Cicognini Academy in Verona during his military service).

In his spare time, Manzù began to draw, paint, and model clay, training his eye and his hand through an

THIS BRONZE SCULPTURE OF *GIULIA ON THE CHAIR* (1966) IS ONE OF A SERIES OF WORKS INVOLVING THE CHAIR THEME; EVEN THE CHAIR WITHOUT A FIGURE BECAME A FAVORITE SUBJECT OF THE ARTIST, AND IS OFTEN REPRESENTED IN LIFE-SIZE SCULPTURES. THE ARDEA COLLECTION FEATURES TWO BRONZE CHAIRS AND TWO SMALL ONES IN GOLD.

IN THE FOREGROUND IS THE BRONZE *RECLINING THEBES* (1983);
IN THE CENTER, THE *LARGE SEATED CARDINAL* (1955)
ON THE LEFT, AND *GIULIA AND MILETO IN THE CARRIAGE (1968)* ON THE RIGHT.

intensive study of Donatello (c. 1386–1466), regarded as the greatest Florentine sculptor prior to Michelangelo. From Donatello's work he learned to reveal the dramatic possibilities of very low relief *(rilievo schiacciato)* and to convey a sense of drama in his religious imagery—the mastery of which is exemplified in his great bronze doors at St. Peter's in Rome and in the Salzburg Cathedral.

A journey to Paris in 1938 proved pivotal for his development as an artist, putting him in contact with the great tradition of French sculpture through the works of Rodin, Maillol, and Degas. Like Rodin and Degas, the movement of a dancing female figure was to inspire Manzù throughout his artistic career.

After his meeting in 1954 with Inge Schabel, a ballerina who posed for him at the Salzburg Sommer-akademie (and who later became his wife), the artist was further inspired to create numerous sculptures on the theme of the dance. Focusing on the dancer's arm movements, Manzù often depicted the ballerina with her arms raised, lifting up her thick mass of hair, or else pulled backwards, touching the ponytail running down her arched back. One of the most graceful versions on this theme is *Dance Step* (1955), a bronze sculpture of a motionless, naked girl, her body thrust forward, straining to balance on the tips of her ballet shoes.

Even as Manzù remained faithful to the human form and some of its most intense forms of self-expression, he also distinguished himself through his powerful drawings and sculptures, many of which were openly critical of Fascism and Nazism. His *Bas-Relief of Christ with a General* (1947) and

THE EPITAPH ON THE ARTIST'S MONUMENTAL TOMBSTONE IN ARDEA READS:
"IN THIS LAND SACRED TO THE MEMORY OF THE RUTULI, CHOSEN AS HIS PRIVILEGED
LAST HOME NEAR HIS WORKS, WHICH KEEP HIS NAME AND RENOWN
ALIVE AND HONORED FOREVER, HERE LIES GIACOMO MANZÙ, 1908–1991."

Bas-Relief with Skeleton (1947–66) in the Ardea Collection, attest to his artistic commitment against war. Both works are a continuation of a theme he began to explore as early as 1939 in his bronze panels of the *Crucifixion* and the *Deposition,* where the dead Christ is shown next to a German general and a prelate, an association that caused quite a stir in both the ecclesiastical and political establishments when they were exhibited in 1941.

In explaining why he repeatedly returned to the theme of war and oppression in his sculpture, Manzù wrote: "I have re-created this series in 1947 as I still believed in the topicality—and topical it is, in my opinion to this very date—of the campaign against militarism that I have incarnated in a general, swollen with stupid and criminal conceit; his antagonist, Christ, symbolizes

humanity, all of us, and foremost of all those who have been and are suffering."

Although the events of the war had forced Manzù in 1942 to leave his teaching post at the Accademia Albertina in Turin, and take refuge at Clusone near Bergamo, by 1943 he had emerged as one of the leading artistic figures in Italy. That year, he was awarded the Grand Prix de Sculpture at the Fourth Quadriennale in Rome, for his nearly life-size bronze nude *Francesca Blanc,* a work that had special meaning for the artist. After the sculpture's installation in the museum at Ardea, Manzù wrote: "It is a work that I still love in a special way. Perhaps on account of the tragic end of the person it portrays, a Ruspoli princess. The abandon of her body was also meant to show a need for protection, an unconscious search for her mother's breast in which to seek refuge as she once did."

An indefatigable talent, Manzù could explore a subject extensively, as in the case of his series of fifty cardinals, a theme that he took up after seeing these prelates in a procession at St. Peter's in 1934. "Their rigid masses made quite an impression on me," he recalls. "They were like a bunch of statues, a series of aligned cubes, and I was seized by an irresistible urge to create in sculpture my own version of that ineffable reality."

The cope (ecclesiastical vestment) of the *Large Seated Cardinal* (1955) is both rigid and imposing, a cone-shaped structure with just a few deep folds; only one hand and the head with its high miter emerge from it. In *Standing Cardinal* (1960) which is over two meters high, Manzù has flattened the cope and the body, and stripped the barely outlined face of its features, as if it were merely a formal link connecting the two cone-shaped forms of which the statue is composed.

After winning the Grand Prix de Sculpture at the 24th Venice Biennale in 1948 along with the English sculptor Henry Moore, Manzù was commissioned by the Vatican to execute the *Fifth Door* of Saint Peter's Basilica in Rome. Fraught with controversy, the complex project did not progress until after the 1958 election of Pope John XXIII. Himself a native of Bergamo, Pope John had met Manzù when he was Archbishop of Venice, and the two had become good friends. Because of the Pontiff's liberal outlook and empathy for the artist, Manzù's new theme of *Death*, for the *Fifth Door* was welcomed, and thus the successful completion of the artist's work was assured.

Drawings for the Vatican's *Portal of Death*, completed in 1964, as well as for *Death of Pope John* (a memorial to the Pope in the door's final version) are included in the collection, showing that, for Manzù, there was a definite continuity between a drawing and a bronze cast. Notes curator Dott.ssa Livia Velani: "Manzù handled bronze as a rough-shaped sheet and obtained from it the same chiaroscuro shades as from a charcoal pencil and the incisive mark of ink."

In the mid-Sixties, following his marriage to Inge Schabel and the birth of his two children, Manzù began a new series of sculptures underscoring the grace and energy of the female figure through his sculptures of the *Lovers*. In this series—of which there are seven examples in the Ardea Collection—the female figure, garbed in rich and heavy drapery, prevails over the nude male in a tension that suspends and encloses the two bodies in space. About this series, Manzù wrote: "Through the close, ongoing embrace of two lovers, I meant to render the unity of two masses that actually interpenetrate until they form a single entity; far from being an inert mass, the image in stone is a concentration of power."

Manzù, who is now buried in the garden of this stunning museum, is rightly considered one of the three major protagonists in the post-war renaissance of Italian sculpture, together with Arturo Martini and Marino Marini. John Rewald confirms this opinion when he writes: "Since the pendulum of history swings from one extreme to another, it is more than possible that this trend of uninhibited freedom will be followed by one which will re-establish closer bonds with nature. New generations will then recognize with gratitude that these bonds were never completely severed, because Giacomo Manzù, in his isolation, kept the classical traditions alive."

Museo Giorgio De Chirico

The Giorgio De Chirico Museum

31 Piazza di Spagna
Rome 00186
Tel: 06/679–6546

**Open Monday through Friday
10:00 A.M. to 1:00 P.M.
Visits only by pre-arranged tours.
There are four tours daily:
10:00 A.M., 10:45 A.M.
11:30 A.M., 12:15 P.M.
Prior booking is essential.**

Bus: 64, 119

THE ENTRANCE TO THE PALAZZO
IS SET OFF BY THE BRONZE
HECTOR AND ANDROMACHE,
CAST IN BRONZE IN 1986.
IT IS BASED ON A SMALLER ORIGINAL
WORK MADE IN 1940.

"In my house overlooking the Piazza di Spagna, I have a magnificent studio which is located on the fifth floor. From its terrace, I can frequently see splendid spectacles in the sky, skies that are clear and skies that are foggy, fiery sunsets, moonlit nights with clouds framed in pale gold, reminiscent of certain seascapes by the Flemish and Dutch masters. My pencil and my colors are always ready, allowing me to record these natural phenomena; such sketches later help me in the execution of my paintings."

This studio, which the painter Giorgio De Chirico (1888–1978) recalls with nostalgia in his *Memoirs,* is on the top floor of an apartment that De Chirico had occupied since 1947. Thanks to the concerted efforts of the Fondazione Giorgio e Isa De Chirico, it is now open for public tours, and provides visitors with a unique opportunity to discover the intimate side of one of the twentieth century's most baffling and controversial artists.

It's an occurrence that likely would have delighted the painter, who after rejecting the Modernist movement and seeing himself as the heir to Titian, was repudiated by the Italian and French avant-garde for essentially the remainder of his life. "The purpose of this museum is to preserve De Chirico's fame, and to assist in new studies of his work, aspects of which are less known to the public," notes docent Barbara Gasperini. "For instance, few people know that he did stage sets for more than thirty operas and plays, including works that were presented at La Scala."

The appeal of this house-museum is not in finding De Chirico's most celebrated works— these are in museums around the world—but in discovering the artist's final home where he resolutely chose to draw, paint, sculpt, and write as he wished, obstinately resisting the accepted shibboleths of his times.

Born in Greece to Italian parents (his father died when he was still a child), De Chirico trained in Athens, Florence, and Munich, where he was influenced by the Symbolist painters Max Klinger and Arnold Böcklin, with their juxtaposition of the commonplace and the fantastic. A painter, sculptor, set designer, and writer, De Chirico is best known as the originator of *Metaphysical Painting*, a term he coined in 1917 with the painter Carlo Carra (1881–1966), when both were patients at the military hospital in Ferrara.

Although the meaning of *Metaphysical Painting* was never precisely defined, the style is characterized by images conveying a sense of haunting mystery and hallucination. This effect was achieved partly through a distorted perspective and artificial lighting, partly by the adoption of a strange iconography which juxtaposed tailors' dummies and statues in place of human figures—a painting aesthetic that resonated throughout the shattered landscape of Europe after the devastation of World War I. In analyzing De Chirico's unique contribution to twentieth-century art, critic Robert Hughes writes: "That De Chirico was a poet, and a great one, is not in dispute. He could condense voluminous feeling through metaphor and association."

While the *Metaphysical Painting* movement was short-lived—De Chirico and Carra quarreled and ended their association in 1919—its

THIS *PENITENT MINOTAUR* IN SILVER METAL WAS CAST IN 1969.

influential effect upon Surrealism soon made it the most talked-about phenomenon of the day, thus establishing De Chirico's international reputation. Hughes goes on to say: "Dali, Ernst, Tanguy and Magritte all came out of early De Chirico, and in the 1920s George Grosz and other German painters used De Chirican motifs to express their vision of an estranged urban world."

The two-story apartment where De Chirico and his Polish-born wife Isabella Farr lived is in the Palazzetto dei Borgognoni, built around 1600. The building takes its name from a celebrated Burgundian family of painters, the Courtois, who resided here during the seventeenth century. As a home and studio, it seems totally in keeping with De Chirico's obdurate rejection of the avant-garde and determined pursuit of his ideal— being an academic painter.

During the years De Chirico lived and worked at the Palazzetto, he was no longer being acclaimed as the ground-breaking iconoclast who

IN THE DINING-ROOM IS A COLLECTION OF STILL-LIFE PAINTINGS
BY THE ARTIST DATING FROM 1934 ONWARD,
A GENRE THAT THE ARTIST LIKED TO DESCRIBE AS *LA VIE SILENCIEUSE*.
NOTE THE PORTRAIT OF DE CHIRICO'S WIFE ISABELLA FARR AS *ISA WITH THE PLUMED HAT*.

had helped to pave the way for the twentieth century's aesthetic revolution. The Surrealists, whom he had so inspired, excoriated him for turning his back on modern art, and for resorting to pastiches of his earlier work. By now, however, De Chirico was railing against the very Modernist movement he had helped to forge, placing it on a par with Fascism and Nazism, as one of the horrors of his time.

One may be tempted to wonder if the artist's reactionary bent toward Modernism also compelled him to live in a home that reflected stolid bourgeois comfort. Certainly the highly polished wood parquet floors, Oriental rugs, and the mix of gilt furniture in the reception rooms make this look more like the residence of a successful lawyer or businessman, than of a nonconformist. However, since he left the furnishing of their home to his wife (being essentially indifferent to such things), it is difficult to be certain.

That De Chirico enjoyed watching cartoon animation and quiz shows with the volume turned all the way down certainly underscores his unorthodox behavior and originality.

"He saw television as an art form," notes docent Barbara Gasperini. "He believed that the mind worked essentially through images, and that television was a source of visual ideas."

On the walls of this house-museum hang classically drawn portraits and self-portraits, nudes, still-lifes with fruit, and seascapes, as well as the paintings of Hellenistic mythology, most of which were

THE PAINTING OVER THE FIREPLACE, *THE BATTLE OF THE GLADIATORS*, WAS PAINTED IN 1969.

De Chirico's 1945 nude self-portrait, which the artist claimed at the time was "the most finished painting I have ever carried out." In reaction to the critics who dismissed his mature work, De Chirico even took to signing his art "Pictor Optimus" ("the best painter"). "He was very narcissistic," observes Gasperini. "The only painter he didn't criticize was Picasso. He was very vain, saying that he was the greatest artist of the twentieth century. I think it was a cover for great timidity."

No painting or sculpture by any other artist was ever displayed in the apartment. When the director of New York's Museum of Modern Art presented him with a book on post-war American painting, *Art in Progress,* he went to the trouble of replacing the cover with his own variant, *Art in Progressive Putrefaction.*

Gasperini believes there still remains "much confusion about De Chirico's art," (part of which he helped to perpetuate). "For one thing there's a problem with dating his work," she explains. "Sometimes, he put an earlier date on paintings that he made in the 1970s. He did this partly to fool people into paying a higher price for them, knowing that his earlier work was more highly prized than paintings he did later in life."

Italian art dealers used to observe wryly that De Chirico's bed must have been six feet off the ground, to hold all the "early work" he kept "discovering" beneath it. (It's interesting to see that the artist actually slept in a monastic single bed, in a room hardly bigger than a broom closet.)

Perplexing in life as well as in death, De Chirico's complex and intractable personality resonates throughout this house-museum. Some think the key to understanding

executed after De Chirico's move to this apartment. Polished gold and silver metal sculptures of seated Muses bearing classical columns and embracing mannequins emulating the posture of warriors depicted on ancient Greek vases also belong to this same period. (Only a handful of paintings touch upon the motifs and compositions characteristic of his painting from his Metaphysical period.)

After abandoning *Metaphysical Painting,* the artist returned to the techniques of the Old Masters, persuaded that the paintings of Titian, Rubens, Van Dyck, Dürer, and Delacroix were vastly superior to any works produced since Impressionism. "He was always going against the tide," Gasperini points out. "When he painted a still-life, he didn't like to think of it as a 'nature morte.' He didn't accept this name. In painting there could be no death. His aim, I think, was to capture the secret life of nature, and put it in his paintings."

The best-known work on display is

THE STUDIO OF THE PAINTER AS HE LEFT IT, WITH HIS LAST UNFINISHED WORK ON THE EASEL. THE TOPS OF THE BOOKCASES ARE DECORATED WITH PLASTER MODELS OF CLASSICAL BUSTS, WHICH OFTEN INSPIRED DE CHIRICO'S SCULPTURES AND PAINTINGS.

De Chirico's intentions is in his studio, which takes up almost an entire floor and is arranged like that of a working artist with paints, brushes, and palettes at the ready, as well as plaster replicas of ancient Roman busts, which he often interpreted in his paintings. An immense easel still bears the unfinished canvas on which he was working before he died: a large study of a reclining bather, based on a detail from a Michelangelo tondo. It is touching to see that a coral tooth and an iron horseshoe were hung on the back of the easel for good luck. "It's important that everything has been left this way," says Gasperini. "You can still feel De Chirico's spirit and presence." Perhaps that is the kind of tribute that even De Chirico might have found satisfying.

Museo Mario Praz

The Mario Praz Museum

Via Zanardelli, N. 1
Rome 00186
Tel: 06/686–1089

Open everyday (except Monday)
9:00 A.M. to 7:00 P.M.
Visits only by pre-arranged
guided tour.

Bus: 64, 119, 280

THE ENTRANCE TO THE
MARIO PRAZ MUSEUM INSIDE
THE PRIMOLI PALACE
CONTAINS THE MONUMENT TO
CHARLOTTE NAPOLEON (LOTTE) PRIMOLI,
THE DAUGHTER OF LUCIEN BONAPARTE.

"I JUDGE those people who are not interested in their homes and who are not moved by the harmony of beautiful furniture, in the same way that Shakespeare judged people who were deprived of musical sensibility—they are born for treason, deception and thievery. Don't put your faith in such men!

"One might reproach me for judging men by their outward appearances and remind me that 'clothes do not make the man.' I would prefer to apply another well-known proverb: 'Style is the man.' In other words, 'Tell me where you live and I will tell you who you are.' Even if a man is deformed, he can still project around him an ideal of harmony and beauty in such a way that his soul can continuously be reflected within it."

So wrote the remarkable aesthete, critic, and collector Mario Praz (1896–1982) in the introduction to his book *History of Interior Decoration.* Praz projected that "ideal of harmony and beauty" onto a creation that at one time was shown only to a privileged few: his apartment in Rome. Unlike most homes in this city, its intention was to embody the prototype of a harmonious interior that was "a museum of the soul, an archive of its experiences."

Even today, the Mario Praz Museum remains one of the best-kept secrets in Rome, familiar mainly to connoisseurs and admirers of Praz, who was not only Italy's most distinguished scholar of English literature, but also a pioneering collector of Neoclassical furniture and art, as well as of nineteenth-century watercolors of interiors. Now that such items are so appreciated, it is difficult to envision to what extent they were neglected during the period when Praz was actively involved in most of his collecting.

To Romans, he was also—to his secret delight—a personality to be feared, as well as respected. Believing he possessed occult powers, some of his neighbors referred to him as "MP," thinking it unlucky to mention his full name. If they saw him on the street, hurrying between antique shops and libraries, they would turn over the coins in their pockets to avert any chance of falling victim to the "evil eye."

While many aesthetes tend to view Praz as a tastemaker and founder of a trend in antique collecting, he regarded himself as the embodiment of European civilization. In the *History of Interior Decoration* he hints at the emotional resonance he found in old pictures and furniture, and how it was strengthened by the destruction he had witnessed during World War II.

A man who spent his honeymoon collecting Roman antiquities, he confessed that objects were more important to him than people, and it is clear that the emotional grip of his collection became greater when his marriage to his Scottish wife, Vivyan, collapsed during World War II. "People betray you, but objects never do," he is reported to have said.

Praz waged a lengthy campaign to persuade the Italian state to buy his collections for a museum that would bear his name. Negotiations had reached an acrimonious impasse upon his death, and the proposal seemed altogether doomed—even after thieves ransacked his flat and made off with the best silver and porcelain, as well as several of his smaller pictures.

It wasn't until 1986 that the state decided to acquire the collection from

Praz's heirs. Stolen items that had reappeared in the antiques market were bought and returned to the apartment. Five years ago, the Mario Praz Museum opened its doors as

AMONG THE TREASURES
IN THIS GALLERY
ARE A MARBLE SCULPTURE OF
CUPID HUNTING
BY ADAMO TADOLINI (CANOVA'S PUPIL),
AND THE HEAD OF
MADAME DE L'HORME BY JOSEPH CHINARD.
THE ROOM'S DECOR AND FURNISHINGS,
INCLUDING THE CHANDELIER
AND AN ARMCHAIR,
WERE INSPIRED BY A PAINTING
OF ISABELLA OF NAPLES,
THE QUEEN MOTHER OF
THE BOURBON KING OF NAPLES

the charming Italian equivalent of the house-museums which had so impressed Praz in his youth: the Nissim de Camondo Museum in Paris and the Sir John Soane Museum in London.

Visitors are taken round on guided tours, which allow one to linger over the statues, busts, wax portraits, pictures, furniture, porcelain, musical

FACING THE DESK OF MARIO PRAZ IS A RARE ERARD HARP.
HE WROTE NUMEROUS BOOKS AT THIS DESK,
WHICH IS ALSO SHOWN IN A PAINTING ON THE WALL BETWEEN THE WINDOWS.

instruments, books, and curios, lovingly arranged in nine rooms. Apart from a small gallery for the rotating display of Praz's collection of watercolors, there is no sense of being in a museum. Despite the breadth of these collections—there are 1,200 objects on display—one never feels overwhelmed or claustrophobic. The overall impression is that of having entered an extrarordinary universe that was lovingly assembled by a consummate collector. A notable example of Praz's passion and erudition is the rare collection of seventeenth- to nineteenth-century wax models of effigies, portraits, busts, and religious or mythological compositions.

The flat, which is on the third floor of the Palazzo Primoli in Via Zanardelli, just to the north of Piazza

THE BEDROOM OF PRAZ'S DAUGHTER LUCIA
CONTAINS FURNISHINGS
FROM BOTH THE EMPIRE AND BIEDERMEIER PERIODS.

Navona, must have been a challenge to arrange, since the high, narrow rooms are awkwardly shaped, forming an enfilade overlooking the street. The objects are presented as Praz left them (he made sketches of each wall so there could be no doubt, and the museum's curatorial staff has remained faithful to his intentions).

A tiny hallway crammed with paintings and books opens onto a lengthy gallery, where the predominant colors and furniture highlight the intimate and accessible Neoclassicism that Praz so loved, "whose full spring came in the France of Louis XVI, whose summer was the Empire of Napoleon, and whose languid autumn the delicious awkwardness of Biedermeier."

Decorated in white and gold, the room takes its inspiration from the painting *The Queen Mother Isabella of Naples at Capodimonte* by the Neapolitan artist Vittoria Abbati (1840). "Praz's home is an extension of this painting," notes curator Dott.ssa Patrizia Rosazza. "He even bought the chandelier and the chair which are depicted in this painting. Even the gold picture hangers are the same."

At the far end of the room is a quite exquisite marble statue of *Cupid Hunting* by Adamo Tadolini (1788–1868), a student of Antonio Canova, which is believed to have once belonged to Louis Bonaparte, the former King of Holland. It so entranced Praz's housekeeper that one day she was discovered tenderly embracing it.

The gallery leads into a brilliant green study, which is filled with French Neoclassical portraits and marble busts, exotic musical instruments, and a French Empire writing desk made of mahogany from the French West Indies, its doors flanked by one-footed griffins. While Praz admired the Greek- and Egyptian-inspired animal motifs used by his favorite furniture designers, such as Thomas Hope, he also believed that the griffins on his writing table showed "the admirable continuity of tradition in the French styles, for the throne of Dagobert I [a seventh-century French monarch] is flanked by similar stylized animals." Sergio De Francisco's 1964 painting of Praz seated at his cherished desk in a cluttered study in the Palazzo Ricci on the Via Giulia (his prior residence) richly illustrates the collector's passions and interests.

THIS INTARSIA-DECORATED BOOKCASE, MADE DURING THE RESTORATION PERIOD IN ITALY, COMES FROM THE MARIGUOLI PALACE IN SPOLETO. IT IS THE RAREST AND MOST PRECIOUS PIECE OF FURNITURE IN THIS HOUSE-MUSEUM.

Praz's desire to replicate the objects from particular paintings hanging in his home is also evident in his study; for instance, he took great pride in purchasing an Erard harp similar to the one in the painting *Young Woman with Harp in an Interior* by Ulysses Griffon (1830).

In his bedroom, which is decorated with framed French eighteenth-century wallpaper panels, pride of place is given to a mahogany Empire bed and an Italian cheval looking glass; on the opposite wall is part of his collection of framed fans. Praz's favorite piece in this room was an elegant Neoclassical chest of drawers containing 325 different marbles and semi-precious stones from all the Tsar's mines throughout the Russian Empire. "Praz cared a great deal for marble," says Rosazza. "It reminded him of the ancient Roman edifices, of the continuum of history, as well as those things that remain of the past."

The library, which is dominated by a fine Neapolitan maple bookcase inlaid with mahogany intarsia—the most valuable piece in the entire house—provides another microcosm of its owner's predilections: Italian and English literature, including the standard Italian translation of Shakespeare, of which Praz was general editor; Praz's own books on Lamb and Byron; his remarkable collection of emblem-books dating back to the Renaissance; along with architectural treatises by Robert Adam and Thomas Hope, as well as Charles Percier and Pierre-Francois-Léonard Fontaine.

Praz may be the only collector to have written a guidebook to his own home. First published in 1958, *The House of Life* is a cross between an autobiography and a guidebook, consisting of a stream of anecdotes told by Praz as he conducts a tour of his apartment in the Via Giulia.

THE GIRAFFE-SHAPED PIANO
IS BY RICHTER;
THE LYRE WAS MADE IN NAPLES IN 1828.

(Recently republished, it provides many fascinating insights into the museum's collections.)

Touring the Mario Praz Museum, one might wonder whether this home was lived in by someone for whom collecting had become an obsession. Yet Praz's scholarship and unique vision of the things he gathered about him throughout his life demonstrates something much more profound. Upon discovering his unique legacy to the City of Rome, we may begin to grasp what he meant when he wrote: "Just as many pieces of furniture are like molds of the human body, empty forms waiting to receive it, . . . so finally the whole room or apartment becomes a mold of the spirit, the case without which the soul would feel like a snail without its shell."

Palazzo Massimo alle
Terme-Museo Nazionale Romano

The National Roman Museum in the Massimo Palace

Largo di Villa Peretti, N.1
Rome 00185
Tel: 06/520–726

Open Tuesday through Saturday 9:00 A.M. to 7:00 P.M.
Open Sunday 9:00 A.M. to 1:00 P.M.
The ticket office closes one hour before the museum. Visits to the second floor to view the mosaics, frescoes, and stucco bas-reliefs take place at set times. Prior booking is necessary for groups and individuals.

Bus: 64. 137, 492, 910
Metro A: Repubblica

ALTHOUGH INSPIRED BY
LATE SIXTEENTH-CENTURY ARCHITECTURE,
THIS STATELY EDIFICE,
DESIGNED BY CAMILLO PISTRUCCI,
WAS COMPLETED IN 1887.
UNTIL 1960, THE SIX-STORY BUILDING
WAS THE SEAT OF THE JESUIT COLLEGE
"MASSIMILIANO MASSIMO,"
WHOSE STUDENTS INCLUDED
THE ARCHITECT CLEMENTE VICI AND
THE WRITER IGNAZIO SILONE.
(ARCHIVIO FOTOGRAPHICO MUSEO NAZIONALE
ROMANO DI PALAZZO MASSIMO)

WHILE ancient Roman easel paintings were once exhibited widely in temples and other public buildings, and huge panels depicting battle scenes were carried in the triumphal processions of victorious generals, none have come down to us today. The only known pictorial works remaining from ancient Rome are frescoes. Among the most remarkable are those that once adorned the *triclinium* (a partially underground living and dining area shielded from the summer's heat) within the villa of Augustus's wife Livia at Prima Porta.

These stunning wall paintings, representing a fantastic *trompe-l'oeil* garden filled with trees such as firs, cypress, pines, oaks, oleander, boxwood, laurel, and fruit trees, including quince, pomegranate, and apple, enlivened by a variety of birds and blooming flowers, not only imparted a sense of spaciousness and grandeur to often cramped quarters, but provided the illusion of a refreshing respite from Rome's heat and humidity. Painted between 10 and 40 B.C., the Roman author Pliny attributed these frescoes to the artist Ludius, who is said to have invented the *trompe-l'oeil* technique; recent scholarship, however, maintains that they were actually derived from Hellenistic scene-painting, and were intended to represent an Oriental paradise.

These entrancing frescoes are among the rarities on display at the recently renovated Palazzo Massimo, a grandiose Neo-Renaissance edifice built between 1883 and 1887.

THESE STUNNING FRESCOES AND FRAGMENTARY STUCCO DECORATIONS
ON THE VAULT EXCAVATED IN 1879
FROM THE ANCIENT AUGUSTAN VILLA OF THE FARNESINA, ARE FROM "CUBICLE B."
THE CENTRAL PANEL DEPICTS APHRODITE SEATED ON A THRONE
WITH ONE OF THE *CARITI* AND A YOUNG EROS.
THE PREDOMINANT THEMES IN THESE ATTIC-STYLE FRESCOES ARE
THE EROTIC ASPECTS OF FEMININITY.

Thanks to an ambitious building restoration and expansion program, this spacious museum now offers an overview of the high points of Roman art and civilization from the late Republican age until the end of the Empire.

Between the second century B.C. and the first century A.D., when Rome established its hegemony over the Mediterranean world, its ruling elite demonstrated a strong preference for Greco-Hellenestic sculpture, a prominent part of this museum's holdings. Such works were either appropriated by Roman generals from cities and religious sanctuaries during their military campaigns, or were the result of a wide-scale production of copies, which were used to decorate public buildings, temples, and imposing residences.

Julius Caesar, himself, was one of the most assiduous collectors of such art, and one of the Palazzo Massimo's prized possessions is an exquisite semi-draped nude which once graced Caesar's gardens in Rome. Known as the *Statue of Niobid from Sallust's Gardens* (the wealthy Roman historian Sallust acquired Caesar's estate after his assassination), it represents one of Niobe's dying daughters straining to remove an arrow from her back. The work (which dates from around 440 B.C., and which may have originally decorated the façade of the temple of Apollo in Euboea, a Greek island in the West Aegean Sea), illustrates the Greek myth of Niobe, who took great pride in her numerous progeny. Resentful of Niobe's boasting, the jealous gods Apollo and Diana took their revenge by slaying

THE *LANCELOTTI DISCUS THROWER* IS ONE OF THE MOST FAMOUS ROMAN COPIES
OF AN ORIGINAL GREEK BRONZE FROM ABOUT 450 B.C.,
DEPICTING AN ATHLETE THROWING A DISCUS.
HISTORICAL TRADITION ATTRIBUTES THE ORIGINAL SCULPTURE TO MYRON,
WHO WAS WELL-KNOWN FOR HIS PORTRAYAL OF ATHLETES IN MOTION.
SENT TO HITLER DURING WORLD WAR II, IT WAS RETURNED TO ITALY IN 1946.
(ARCHIVIO FOTOGRAPHICO MUSEO NAZIONALE ROMANO DI PALAZZO MASSIMO)

her children with bow and arrows.

When unable to acquire Greek originals, the members of the ancient Roman aristocracy commissioned statuary from Hellenistic artists who had emigrated to Rome in search of wealthy patrons. One outstanding example of such work is the striking full-length marble portrait statue known as *The General of Tivoli*, regarded as one of the most important sculptures in the final phase of the Republic.

Found among the ruins of the Temple of Hercules the Victor at Tivoli, it depicts an older man from the ruling class, perhaps a general who participated in the victorious Roman campaigns in Asia Minor between 90 and 70 B.C. Typical of late Hellenistic statuary, whose parts were sculpted separately and then put together, its body epitomizes the heroic nudity of Greek statuary, whereas its battle-weary face and piercing gaze underscore the realistic tradition of Italic art.

The refined and emotive powers of such Greek sculptors as Praxiteles, Phidias, and Myron were not lost upon the Roman Emperors, as evidenced by some of the stunning archaeological finds in this museum. In some instances, these were original Greek works, as with *The Maid of Anzio* (found in the gallery of Nero's seaside villa at Anzio), a delicately featured young priestess wearing a diaphanous garment and bearing a tray of objects most likely connected to the Cult of Dionysus, the god of wine and the vine.

They also collected fine Hellenistic copies including such works as the *Crouching Aphrodite,* which once graced the baths at Hadrian's Villa in Tivoli, the powerful and idealized *Lancelotti Discus Thrower,* the sensuous *Sleeping Hermaphrodite,* and a particularly rare bronze statue of

THIS VEILED PORTRAIT
OF HADRIAN'S WIFE SABINA
IS CONSIDERED TO HAVE BEEN MADE
FOLLOWING HER DEATH
AND DEIFICATION.
IT REVEALS THE STRONG INFLUENCE
THAT IDEALIZED GREEK PORTRAITURE
HAD ON THE ART
OF HADRIAN'S PERIOD.

Dionysus, the god of fertility and wine.

The deification of Augustus (ruled 27 B.C.–A.D. 14), spurred the creation of many sculptural portraits of the emperor, his family, and his inner circle, a form of political propaganda which continued until the fall of the Empire. The museum shows the development of the portrait bust, whose variety, realism, and elements of self-assurance have had a major impact on Western art. These marble busts not only demonstrate the Romans' veneration for the family and its ancestors, but also their preference for unbiased realism. While many such portrait busts were intended to demonstrate a ruler's benevolent authority, others convey

surprising malevolence. For instance, an exceptional tiny portrait bust of Caligula reveals his cruelty, while the head of a frowning and ferocious Caracalla emphasizes his brutish nature.

Roman artists also had great expertise in the handling of inlay decorations *(opus sectile)* made with finely cut pieces of marble, stone, and even colored glass. Two panels from the Basilica of Giunio Basso, a consul in A.D. 331 (found on the wall of a large hall which was the private basilica in a residence on the Esquiline), demonstrate the great luxury that characterized urban aristocratic residences from this period.

One inlaid panel illustrates the myth of Hercules's companion Hylas being abducted by nymphs, while the other shows the beginning of a race at the circus. Discovered during the fifteenth century, they were seen and drawn by the artist Giuliano da Sangallo, who described them as *cosa meravigliosa* ("a thing of wonder"). Indeed they are.

The museum's vast numismatic collection (reputed to be among the largest in the world), is handsomely displayed in steel-and-glass cases, each equipped with a sliding magnifying glass that permits viewers to examine each coin in great detail. Scholars maintain that the Roman currency, known as *denarii,* was used to promulgate the differing values and symbols of the democratic party *(populares)* and the aristocratic party *(optimates).* Images of Venus were chosen to represent the *optimates,* whereas those of Apollo were used on coins minted by the *populares.* The latter used coinage to popularize their programs, which included agrarian reform, public works, cancellation of debts, and the promise of free distribution of corn.

According to the museum's exhibition, all coins in the Roman Empire (with the exception of pieces in heavy bronze, which were struck by hand), were engraved directly onto dies by specialized craftsmen. After the dies were tempered by heating, they were then handed to workmen charged with stamping them. The finished coins were struck by hammering prepared metal blanks. After the coins had been checked for fraud by local magistrates, they were then put into circulation.

Banks were established in Rome as early as the fourth century B.C., when the butchers in the main city square were replaced by money changers in order to heighten the status and dignity of the Forum. In time, the money changers became specialized bankers; not only did they set up an efficient cashier service, they also

THIS MOSAIC FROM NERO'S PALACE IN ANZIO ONCE DECORATED HIS *NYMPHAEUM*.
THE CENTRAL NICHE REPRESENTS A RECLINING HERCULES, RESTING AFTER HIS LABORS.

intervened in the collection of loaned capital both within and outside of Rome. One of the oldest services was accepting and safe-guarding deposits, which could be either interest-bearing or not. People could even take out small loans, provided they put up the collateral, which would usually be an object of some value.

The bankers of Rome seem to have conducted a flourishing business in the Forum, for they knew the exchange rates throughout the Empire and would take money on deposit, and provide a draft on foreign banks. When Cicero's son was sent to the University of Athens, he did not travel with a chest of money, as would become necessary later, in the Middle Ages, but with a letter of credit payable in Athens.

Viewing this outstanding collec-tion of art and artifacts, visitors will be able to better appreciate the profound impact of Roman civiliza-tion upon our present-day world. This museum demonstrates that the Empire's ruling elite was as image-conscious as heads-of-state are today, and commissioned works of art and coinage that were intended to enhance their popularity and prestige.

While one may reasonably reflect upon the balance between the investment made and the returns achieved—particularly in light of the ultimate collapse of the Roman Empire—there is no denying the powerful effect of certain glorious artifacts of its culture, particularly those examples now so artfully presented at the Palazzo Massimo alle Terme.

Museo Napoleonico

The Napoleonic Museum

**Piazza DiPonte Umberto, N. 1
Rome 00186
Tel: 06/688-06286**

**Open Tuesday through Sunday
9:00 A.M. to 7:00 P.M.**

Bus: 64, 119, 280

THE LAUREL-CROWNED
HEAD OF NAPOLEON REPRESENTING HIM
AS A ROMAN SENATOR
DOMINATES THE ENTRANCE TO
THE MUSEUM.

I T is among the great ironies of history that one of Rome's most fervent admirers, as well as one of its greatest opponents, could wage war against the Papal States, yet yearn on his deathbed that members of his family marry into the great Italian dynasties that gave Christianity its popes. While helping himself to scores of artworks from the Vatican to stock the Louvre Museum in Paris, he also ordered an ambitious restoration program of the city's ancient monuments. He named his heir the future King of Rome, yet he himself never managed to visit the Eternal City. Such a man was Napoleon Bonaparte (1769–1821).

This phenomenal love-hate relationship with Rome, which coursed through Napoleon's meteoric career, is extensively documented in one of the city's most intriguing, yet lesser-known institutions, the Napoleonic Museum, created by Giuseppe Primoli and left to the city in 1927. Born in 1851, Primoli was a descendant of the Roman line of the Bonaparte family through his mother, Carlotta Bonaparte. Wed to Pietro Primoli, Count of Foglia, Carlotta had dual ties to the Bonapartes: her father was the son of Lucien Bonaparte, Prince of Canino, while her mother, Zenaïda Bonaparte, was the daughter of Joseph Bonaparte, King of Naples and Sicily (1806–1808), later King of Spain and the Indies (1808–1813).

Primoli spent his childhood and youth at the court of Napoleon III and the Empress Eugénie, during his sojourn in France between 1853 and 1870. While obtaining his law degree, he frequented the literary salon of his aunt Mathilde Bonaparte, becoming the intimate of the poet Prosper Mérimée (who wrote the novella on which is based Georges Bizet's opera *Carmen*), the literary critic Charles-Augustin Sainte-Beuve, as well as of the novelists Gustave Flaubert and Guillaume de Maupassant.

The fall of Napoleon III and the Second Empire after France's defeat in the Franco-Prussian War signified the end of Primoli's world as he knew it. Returning to Rome, he spent the rest of his days reconstructing the public and private history of Napoleon and the Bonaparte dynasty. Thanks to his close ties with Mathilde Bonaparte and the Empress Eugénie, he was able to acquire rare and precious objects for his collection, including a suite of furniture by Jacob upholstered in red damask from Napoleon's apartments in the château of St. Cloud, Winterhalter's famous portraits of Napoleon III and Eugénie in court dress, and the marriage contract between Napoleon and Marie-Louise of Austria.

The portraits, statues, furnishings, mementos, and political cartoons at the Napoleonic Museum underscore the mystique of Bonaparte, an impoverished young nobleman of Corsican parentage who rose to become Emperor of the French at thirty-four. Still, the singularity and appeal of this collection comes from the manner in which it reveals the private side of the Bonapartes, in all their grandeur and foibles. It is here that visitors can see a hopeful drawing that "St. Napoleon" made for his mother, who (like any good Italian mother) felt that nothing was too exalted for her son. It is also here that one can admire the sumptuous red velvet court dress and train that once belonged to Napoleon's mother, Letizia Ramolino Bonaparte, as well

THIS SMALL BISCUIT PORCELAIN
BUST OF NAPOLEON IS
SURROUNDED BY
A COLLECTION OF POCKET-WATCHES
FROM THE PERIOD.

as a board game sent to Napoleon to help him forget his incarceration on St. Helena.

Even if history did not allow Napoleon's son to rule as King of Rome, almost all of the members of Bonaparte's family lived at one point in Rome both before and after Waterloo. After her son's defeat and exile, Letizia obtained asylum from Pope Pius VII in Rome, staying at the Palazzo Venezia until her death in 1836. (She had already lived in Rome as early as 1804, as the guest of her half-brother Cardinal Fesch, at that time minister-plenipotentiary to Italy.) Through her marriage to Prince Camillo Borghese in 1803, Napoleon's sister Pauline lived in Rome, first in a seventeenth-century villa which has since become the Galleria Borghese, then in the Villa Bonaparte, near the Porta Pia.

THE TWO SMALL BUSTS ARE OF
LETIZIA MURAT (THE DAUGHTER OF CAROLINE BONAPARTE), AND HER SON ACHILLES.
THE "IRON JEWELRY" FROM BERLIN,
WHICH WAS WORN WHEN WOMEN SOLD THEIR JEWELS TO RAISE MONEY FOR
THE WAR EFFORT, BELONGED TO CAROLINE, AS DID THE MINIATURE WITH HER PORTRAIT.

Louis Bonaparte, King of Holland, and his wife, Hortense de Beauharnais (Josephine's daughter), as well as their son Louis-Napoleon (the future Napoleon III) also sojourned in Rome, as did Joseph's wife Julie Clary, accompanied by her daughters Zenaïda and Charlotte.

Although Napoleon never personally reached Rome, that did not deter him from sending troops to occupy it on repeated occasions. One exhibit devoted to the repeated subjugation of Rome by the French illustrates how Napoleon's army, under the command of General Berthier, occupied the city on February 9, 1798. (The pretext for the invasion was the papal troops' gunning down of the French General Duphot.)

Inspired by the momentum of the French Revolution, the Roman crowd demanded a republic. On the night of February 20, two men entered the Quirinal apartments of Pope Pius VI (1775–99) and demanded his renunciation of temporal power. Despite his advanced age (he was eighty-two) and his frailty, the Pope refused. The Fisherman's Ring was then pulled from his finger and he was hustled into a carriage out of Rome, and forcibly extradited to France, where he died the following year.

Rome's short-lived republic fell less than a year later on September 18, 1799, with the intervention of the Neapolitan armies of King Ferdinand IV. The new Pope Pius VII, elected at the conclave in Venice, held on March 14, 1800, entered Rome in early July. A drawing by Tommaso Mercandetti, intended for a commemorative medal, shows the papal cortege in the Piazza del Popolo.

Four years later, Napoleon asked the Pope to officiate at his coronation in 1804 at Notre-Dame in Paris. (While himself an agnostic, Napoleon realized that the excesses against the clergy had undermined the French Revolution, and so had restored the Church in France.) Yet, when the French army won the battles of Urbino and Ancona in 1808, Napoleon proclaimed the Papal States to be part of the French Empire and Rome a free Imperial City with the Pope as its bishop.

Pius VII responded by excommunicating Napoleon. The Emperor then ordered the arrest of the Pope. In the early hours of the morning of July 6, 1809, French soldiers quietly overpowered the Papal Guard, and ordered the Pope into a carriage, without even giving him the time to

THIS VITRINE CONTAINS MINIATURES OF THE BONAPARTE FAMILY, INCLUDING ONE OF NAPOLEON'S MOTHER.

take money or his spectacles. There followed six terrible years of humiliations, including house arrest at Fontainebleau, but by the end of that time, Napoleon was exiled to St. Helena, and Pius VII, then aged

A MARBLE COPY OF CANOVA'S ORIGINAL BUST OF PAULINE BONAPARTE, WHO WAS CELEBRATED FOR HER BEAUTY AND HER GENEROSITY TOWARD HER BROTHER WHEN HE WAS SENT INTO EXILE.

seventy-four, returned in triumph to the Piazza del Popolo, an event commemorated by a period engraving in the museum. What is most amazing of all is that although he had been bullied by Napoleon, Pius VII never forgot that Napoleon had restored Catholicism in France and so magnanimously took the entire Bonaparte family under his wing.

Another exhibit is devoted to Napoleon's sister, Pauline Bonaparte, who may be best remembered for having posed for Antonio Canova's celebrated statue, reclining as Venus upon an Empire couch, now displayed in the Borghese Gallery. Even in an age when nudity was rather fashionable, this statue was thought to be rather daring, except by Pauline. When one of her friends asked how she could have posed almost naked, she casually replied: "Oh, there was a stove in the studio."

Among the objects Primoli collected that were linked to Pauline were a dressing-table, a couch that resembles the one she posed on for Canova, a copy of a small bust by Canova, and a Canova's mold of her breast. Although she was nicknamed "Notre Dame des colifichets" ("Our Lady of the knick-knacks"), most historians agree that she was the most loyal of Napoleon's siblings. When he was imprisoned on Elba, she gave him all her jewels and went to live with him on the island.

A set of baby teeth, a pair of delicate miniatures painted by Jean-Baptiste Isabey of Marie-Louise and her infant son, the King of Rome, along with a tender painting by A.V. Sixdeniers of *Napoleon in His Study with the King of Rome,* pay homage to Napoleon II (1811–1832). Virtually unknown to the French until Sarah Bernhardt's interpretation in Edmond Rostand's *L'Aiglon,* he was never allowed to live in Rome, but instead was named Duke of Reichstadt and was condemned to live in exile at the palace of Schönbrunn, near Vienna. No one even worried about marrying him off: an engraving in the museum shows the young scion struck down with tuberculosis and lying on his death-bed. (The illness killed him when he was twenty-two-years-old.) In December 1940, his remains were sent to France at the behest of the German Chancellor Adolf Hitler, and entombed opposite Napoleon's own monumental tomb.

Passing from room to room,

visitors are able to follow the births, marriages, and complex relationships among the various Bonapartes, and gain a more comprehensive overview of this exceptional family. Thanks to Giuseppe Primoli's fascination with his Bonapartist heritage, this museum sheds new light on one of history's most intriguing and controversial personalities, as well as upon the other members of his extensive family.

THIS ELABORATE GOLDEN PORTAL
CAME FROM
THE CHURCH OF SANTO SPIRITO IN SASSIA,
DEMOLISHED AT THE BEGINNING
OF THE 1900S.

Museo delle Navi Romane di Fiumicino

The Museum of the Roman Ships at Fiumicino

Via A. Guidoni, N. 35
Fiumicino Airport 00050
Tel: 06/652–9192

**Open from Tuesday through Sunday
9:30 A.M. to 1:30 P.M.;
Tuesday and Thursday
2:30 P.M. to 4:30 P.M.
On the first Saturday and last Sunday of every month a guided tour of the archaeological area of Portus departs from the museum at 9:30 A.M. (For all other dates, prior reservation is required.)**

**By train: Take the train from Termini Train Station to Fiumicino-Leonardo da Vinci Airport, then a five-minute cab ride to the museum.
By car: Take the Rome Airport Highway to Via A. Guidoni.**

M OST visitors to Rome who arrive at the Leonardo da Vinci International Airport in Fiumicino, would be surprised to learn that the surrounding airfields were once the site of the greatest man-made harbor in antiquity. Known as the Port of Claudius or simply as Portus ("port" in Latin), the construction of this artificial harbor was initiated by the Emperor Claudius in A.D. 46, after the old harbor of Ostia had begun to silt up with river-borne deposits from the Tiber.

Because of the enormous expense involved in such an operation, the

THIS SIMPLE, MODERN EDIFICE,
FIVE MINUTES FROM
THE LEONARDO DA VINCI AIRPORT,
HARBORS IMPORTANT
ARCHAEOLOGICAL DISCOVERIES:
THE HULLS OF ANCIENT ROMAN SHIPS THAT
WERE ONCE USED
TO TRANSPORT OLIVE OIL, GRAINS,
AND MARBLE TO THE CAPITAL.

THIS PHOTOGRAPH WAS TAKEN DURING THE 1959 EXCAVATION
OF AN ANCIENT ROMAN FISHING BOAT.

plan to build such a harbor was not well-received. Yet, despite these reservations, a site was chosen three kilometers north of the Tiber's mouth. Half the harbor's basin was excavated on dry land, after which two long moles were extended out into the open sea, reaching out like pincers to embrace the wide expanse of water. The harbor was finished only in A.D. 64 under Nero, who commemorated this feat with a specially minted coin.

In its heyday, the circular harbor spanned nearly a third of a mile, and had a canal leading to the Tiber to facilitate the transshipment of goods.

The interior of the port was ringed with quays where ships could be tied to mooring blocks. A lighthouse built on the port's western side used for its foundation the scuttled 1,000-ton ship that Caligula had commissioned to transport his 25.5-meter-high obelisk from Alexandria. This obelisk is now in Saint Peter's Square.

Archaeologists discovered traces of the harbor's ancient stone piers and concrete jetties in 1957, during the airport's construction. Little did they suspect that a year later, they would recover the vestiges of a Roman freighter (*oneraria* in Latin), and three similar vessels the following year, as well as two other unrelated hull fragments. Another hull from a smaller boat was excavated in 1965.

displayed on supporting steel frames inside the Museum of Roman Ships, which was opened to the public in November 1979. Four of the hulls were once part of flat-bottomed cargo ships, (c. A.D. 300–400), whereas the

THESE ANCIENT ROMAN VESSELS
ONCE TRAVELED AS FAR AS ALEXANDRIA, EGYPT,
ONE OF THE MANY PORTS FREQUENTED BY
THESE TRANSPORT FREIGHTERS AT THE ZENITH OF THE ROMAN EMPIRE.
THE MAPS ON THE WALL INDICATE
THE PORTS AROUND THE WORLD WHERE SIMILAR SHIPS
HAVE BEEN UNEARTHED.

All five wrecks were found abutting the right mole of the harbor, in a marginal area of its basin, which was particularly susceptible to silting. The Rome Archaeological Superintendency, which uncovered the startling finds, presumes that in ancient times this area must have been a sort of "cemetery," where boats and ships too old or in too poor a condition to sail were abandoned.

Today, the blackened wooden hulls of these five vessels are handsomely

fifth hull once belonged to a fishing boat (c. A.D. 100) that had been propelled by oars.

If these ancient hulls have survived for so many centuries, it is because they were waterlogged and subsequently buried beneath the harbor's silt deposits. Their blackened appearance is a result of carbonization activated by microorganisms within the various sedimentary layers. Through the use of a mixture of resins applied to their surface, the hulls were protected from further degradation before their installation in the museum.

This exceptional collection of vessels not only enriches our understanding of the various ship types used during the Imperial period, but also allows us to appreciate the construction methods used by ancient shipwrights. Technical historians believe that the outer shell of wooden planks was constructed directly after the boat's keel had been laid. The vessel's internal skeleton was inserted only later, to function as an internal support (the so-called "shell-first" method of construction).

Joinery between planking consisted of tenons (thin tongues of hardwood), which were inserted into apposite grooves cut within the thickness of each plank. The tenons were then locked with pegs or treenails. This way, the self-supporting internal planking strengthened the structure longitudinally and protected the hull from the cargo, typically composed of terra-cotta amphorae (also displayed in the museum). The anchor was the most important piece of equipment on board, and usually a vessel had several of various sizes.

The mast step used to seat the foot of the mast demonstrates that these vessels had been fitted with a single square sail. A pump to remove bilge water was located in a socket within the crutches flanking the mast step. The main sail, the "velum," was made of either linen or hemp, and was sewn from several expanses of cloth. The sails of freighters and transports were generally white, whereas those of warships were red, and sometimes featured ornamental paintings.

The elegant, angular form of one cargo ship made it suitable for small- and medium-range coastal navigation at sea, given its comparatively modest dimensions. The three other cargo vessels, while sharing similar construction characteristics, have rather flat, wide hulls, which indicate that they must have been used for river transport. It is likely that these boats were towed by oxen along the river bank, according to a propulsion system known as tracking, which was still used along the Tiber in the nineteenth century.

The fishing boat, a unique find in itself, featured a central compartment within which the fresh catch was kept alive, thanks to a system that allowed sea water to flood the cavity through stoppered holes along the bottom hull's planking.

If the outskirts of Imperial Rome had the largest port unloading the greatest amount of tonnage in the Mediterranean, it was with good reason. The city needed 500,000 to 600,000 tons of grain a year to produce flour for bread, and local farmers could only provide 150,000 tons of the requisite amount. Up to 450,000 tons of grain had to be imported from the different provinces of the Empire to make up the shortfall. The Romans solved this problem by building a large fleet of grain transports, an achievement that turned out to be as significant as their building of towns, harbors, streets, and aqueducts.

The *onerariae* that they built had large hulls, each of which was capable of carrying up to 1,500 tons of grain. These super freighters (*mirabilis navis*) were no longer constructed after the collapse of the Roman Empire, and would not be built again until the *end* of the eighteenth century.

Most of the freighters sailed to Egypt, which was the principal granary of the Roman Empire. The journey from the Tiber to Alexandria could take between two to three weeks, depending upon the winds.

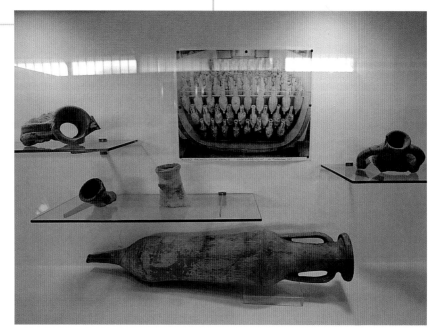

The ships would spend the winter in Alexandria, and it was only after the festival *"Navigium Isidis"* (honoring the goddess of navigation), celebrated on March 5, that the ships would set sail back to Rome.

Knowing well the perils of the sea, the Romans arranged to have a grain fleet of about one hundred ships sail together, to guarantee that enough grain would reach the capital. Out of every four freighters leaving the harbor, on average only three arrived at their final destination. This is one reason why a sailor was called a *mortis socius* ("a companion of death").

By referring to written sources, as well as through the study of iconogra-phy, sailing gear, and the remains of amphorae and food from shipwrecks, it is possible to reconstruct the manner in which sailors lived afloat. Hand grindstones reveal that they were able to make flour from grains, including cornmeal for porridge and breads. The crew's provisions were stored in baskets, sacks, or amphorae. Supplies for an ocean voyage included drinking water, wine, oil, and *garum* (fish paste), as well as cereals, olives, fresh or dried fruit, legumes, smoked and salted meats.

Medicines against seasickness were common, while coins and scales were used for commercial transactions, once the sailors reached dry land. For

THESE MARBLE BUILDING BLOCKS
WERE BROUGHT TO ROME BY SHIP FROM
DISTANT QUARRIES IN THE EMPIRE.

illumination they depended upon oil lamps. While at sea, the crew would be involved in maintenance activities as well, judging by the bone needles that were used to repair sails, and the nets used for fishing, which enriched their modest food supply. Religious customs were also observed by the mariners, with the assistance of portable altars and images of the divinities.

Behind the museum is an ancient building (c. second century A.D.), made of brickwork and tufa blocks, which still contains traces of painted decoration. While its function remains unclear, it most likely was a service building located at the end of the harbor's basin. If a visitor elects to take part in a guided tour, it is also possible to explore the archaeological area of Monte Giulio, which offers an impressive overview of most of the former Claudian port basin where the ruins of other structures have been uncovered, including a cistern, some public baths, and several storage buildings.

Gazing upon the scant remains of the Port of Claudius, one cannot help feeling both reflective and moved by the realization that the greatest ancient port in the Mediterranean now lies beneath Italy's largest and most modern airport.

Museo Nazionale Etrusco di Villa Giulia

The National Etruscan Museum in the Villa Giulia

Piazzale di Villa Giulia, N. 9
Rome 00186
Tel: 06/320–1951

Open Tuesday through Saturday
9:00 A.M. to 2:00 P.M.
Open Wednesday
9:00 A.M. to 7 P.M.
Open Sunday and holidays
9:00 A.M. to 1:00 P.M.

Bus: 90, 90b, 120, 204, 225, 495, 926

Tearoom on premises.

T H E most perfect extant example of the Renaissance conception of a house and garden as an inseparable entity is to be found ten minutes from the Piazza del Popolo, in a valley between the hills of Parioli and the Pincio. Built between 1551 and 1555 for Pope Julius III, it is known simply as the Villa Giulia. To erect this unique residence, the pontiff enlisted an exceptional team, including the painter, architect, and art critic Giorgio Vasari (1511–1574), the Florentine sculptor and architect Bartolomeo Ammannati (1511–1592), and the architect Jacopo Barozzi da Vignola (1507–1573).

THE VILLA GIULIA WAS BUILT MAINLY
BY TWO OF THE LEADING ARCHITECTS OF THE RENAISSANCE,
BARTOLOMEO AMMANNATI AND JACOPO BAROZZI DA VIGNOLA
(ALTHOUGH GIORGIO VASARI TOOK MOST OF THE CREDIT
IN HIS *LIVES OF THE ARTISTS*).

AMMANNATI'S *NYMPHAEUM* WAS INSPIRED BY THOSE IN MANY ANCIENT ROMAN VILLAS.
ONLY TWO STATUES IN THE LARGEST NICHES ARE LEFT, THOSE REPRESENTING
THE RIVER GODS *ARNO* AND *TIBER*,
WHICH ARE FRAMED BETWEEN A SERIES OF DORIC PILASTERS AND,
ABOVE, BY A BORDER OF TRIGLYPHS AND METOPES.

In addition to having the assistance of a small army of craftsmen, painters, and stucco-workers in creating the lavish decor of carved wooden ceilings inlaid with gold, painted friezes, frescoes, and illusionistic trellises of vines, roses, and jasmine on the vault of the villa's semicircular portico, the three architects were advised by Michelangelo himself, whom the Pope had appointed as a consultant to the project.

While Vasari credited himself with the villa's overall design, architectural historians have since established that most of what we see today was the work of Ammannati and Vignola. While the façade appears to be a solid Renaissance edifice, the building was in fact conceived as a "screen" shielding three consecutive courtyards. In the middle courtyard, curved stairs lead down to a sunken courtyard, known as a *nymphaeum*, where the caryatids were originally surrounded by ten putti spouting water from the niches. (Although this *nymphaeum* was the first of its kind, it soon became incorporated into the design of many sixteenth-century Italian villas.)

Between the curved stairs, a secret grotto provided a cool resting place in summer, while a hidden spiral staircase led to the upper loggia and gardens beyond. When the weather became particularly steamy, the Pope and his entourage rested in the small underground rooms next to the grotto that were specifically designed

FELICE BARNABEI'S BUST STANDS LIKE A SENTINEL
NEXT TO ONE OF THE WINGS OF THE MUSEUM HE FOUNDED IN 1889.
NEARBY IS A RECONSTRUCTED ETRUSCO-ITALIAN TEMPLE FROM ALATRI,
A TOWN A FEW MILES NORTH OF ROME.

for coolness, similar to those that were built in the classical villas of ancient Rome.

This extravagant, garlic-eating pontiff, who was a lover of parties, banquets, theater, horse races, and bullfights, usually retired to his villa on hot summer days, sailing up the Tiber from the Vatican in a sumptuous boat bedecked with flowers, in the company of cardinals, dignitaries, and friends. Although Julius never spent a single night in the villa—malaria rendered such estates unhealthy in summer, since their pools and irrigation tanks were breeding grounds for mosquitoes—that didn't stop him from spending a fortune on making it one of the most dazzling estates in Rome.

An indefatigable builder and collector, he saw to it that the garden courtyards were filled with contemporary and ancient statues, and furnished with urns and vases filled with fragrant lemon and orange trees. Yet the pontiff's days in this idyllic setting were abruptly truncated, since he died the very year of the villa's completion. Soon after, Pope Paul IV emptied Villa Giulia of its treasures, taking one hundred and sixty boatloads of statues from the villa to the Vatican.

Over the ensuing centuries, Villa Giulia became a residence for illustrious papal guests, including Sweden's Queen Christina, and later alternated as a hospital, a gunpowder magazine, and a military warehouse. At last, thanks to the concerted efforts of the renowned archaeologist Felice Barnabei, the former villa was transformed and expanded into the Etruscan Museum, which opened in 1889. Its outstanding collections consist primarily of pre-Roman art and objects found in Etruscan tombs or at temple sites in Etruria, an area north of Rome between the Tiber and the Arno rivers (now modern Tuscany and Umbria).

Prior to the rise of Rome, the Etruscans had the most advanced civilization in Italy, one which flourished from 700 to 100 B.C., when their confederation of city-states was conquered by the Romans. Modern research tends to corroborate the Greek historian Herodotus's account that the Etruscans migrated to Italy from Lydia in Asia Minor in the twelfth century B.C. While their alphabet, derived from Greek, can be easily read, their language has never been fully deciphered.

The political and economic apogee of the Etruscans was around 500 B.C., when they were a great maritime power with colonies on Corsica, Elba, Sardinia, the Balearic Islands, and the coast of Spain. Their wealth and power was based partly on trade and partly on their knowledge of mining the iron and copper deposits that were abundant in Etruria. Highly skilled metalworkers and potters, the Etruscans produced some of the finest bronze and goldwork in the ancient world as well as stunning black pottery (*bucchero*), several examples of which are in the museum. (Their technology was so advanced that they were said to have invented the chariot, or *biga*, and introduced it into Italy.)

Thanks to their close ties with the Greek world, the Etruscans became skilled in soldering, casting, sculpting, and painting, all of which had a profound influence on their art. (Slavery and serfdom were important components of the Etruscan economy, and many ceramics workshops were operated by highly specialized slaves, who signed each vase with a personal stamp.)

Like the pharaohs and nobility of Egypt, the Etruscans believed in an afterlife, and prepared for it by decorating their tombs with lively frescoes, and making certain they would be buried with valuable possessions and household objects, including arms, jewelry, toilet accessories, even kitchen equipment. Unlike the Egyptians, however, the Etruscans did not embalm the dead, but instead had their ashes placed in urns or caskets, made either of bronze, terra-cotta, or stone. A hut-shaped bronze funerary urn found in Vulci that illustrates this practice, reveals that Etruscan houses had an oval floor plan and wooden beams.

The museum's comprehensive collection of bronze and iron objects confirms the sophistication of Etruscan civilization. The extensive displays include candelabra, cauldrons, fire-irons, pokers, tongs, grills, a horse bit, helmets, strigils, as well as a two-wheeled chariot with bronze decorations, and curious cage-like bags that athletes used to hold the sand they rubbed on their bodies prior to a sporting event.

A vast and varied array of kitchen and cooking implements demonstrates the importance that Etruscans assigned to both food preparation and dining. Any occasion was an opportune one for a banquet, even during ceremonies honoring the dead. A fresco inside a tomb at Orvieto shows the complicated preparation of such a meal, with the cook and his assistants working to the sound of music provided by a flute. A slave appears to be making a sauce with pounded herbs, cheese, and garlic, mixed with oil, which today we would assume to be *pesto*. Eggs, black grapes, and pomegranates are also depicted, along with biscuits and sweets piled high in pyramids.

Paintings and statues also show that Etruscan men and women reclined together on couches when they dined (a practice much frowned upon in Republican Rome, where a woman sat humbly in the presence of her husband). Such a custom is beautifully extolled in the sarcophagus of the *Bride and Bridegroom*, discovered by Professor Barnabei in the necropolis of Cerveteri, the most important Etruscan city from the seventh to the fourth century B.C.

This double sarcophagus in polychromatic terra-cotta, made at the end of the sixth century B.C., portrays a young man and woman who appear to be attending their own funeral banquet. Their tender expressions and the young man's affectionate gesture of resting his arm and hand protectively against his wife's shoulder, make it one of the most moving sculptures from the ancient world.

While there is much to admire in this exceptional sarcophagus, most visitors would agree that the collection's greatest treasures are the sculptures from the temple dedicated to Minerva, uncovered in the sanctuary of Portonaccio at Veio, seventeen kilometers north of Rome. Even in their damaged state, the celebrated figures of *Apollo and Hercules,* colossal statues in polychrome terra-cotta, exude an exceptional intensity and vitality. It is thought that they were placed confronting each other, on the apex of the temple's roof, at the end of the sixth century B.C. Presumably they were the central figures of a foursome, representing the struggle for the Ceryneian Hind (a golden-horned deer, sacred to Minerva).

The story of Hercules's and Apollo's struggle for the hind is Greek, so is the Archaic expression on their faces. Yet, these sculptures are thought to be the work of Vulca, the famous Etruscan artist from Veio, who is said to have been summoned to Rome by Tarquinius Superbus

THESE ELONGATED BRONZE VOTIVE FIGURES FROM THE VOLTERRA REGION
WERE MADE DURING THE FOURTH AND THIRD CENTURIES B.C.,
AND ARE REMINISCENT OF WORK BY THE TWENTIETH-CENTURY ITALIAN SCULPTOR,
ALBERTO GIACOMETTI.

THIS FAMED BRIDAL COUPLE
IN POLYCHROME TERRA-COTTA
WAS DISCOVERED IN CERVETERI
BY FELICE BARNABEI,
WHO PAINSTAKINGLY PIECED IT TOGETHER,
THUS RESURRECTING
ONE OF THE WORLD'S GREATEST
SCULPTURES.

to execute the statue and decorations for the Capitoline temple of Jupiter. There is something cruelly savage about these sculptures, particularly in the ferociously grinning Medusa's head on the polychrome antefix from the temple, also in the exhibition. What a contrast with the figure of Latona, tenderly holding the infant Apollo in her arms, a work which apparently was executed by the same sculptor. (Latona was the Latin name for the Greek mythological figure Leto, who conceived twins by Zeus,

namely Apollo and Diana, much to the displeasure of his wife Hera.)

Ferocity and delicacy, sensuality and grace, inventiveness and refinement, are all characteristics to be found in the amazing art and culture of the Etruscans. Thanks to the rich and varied exhibits in the Etruscan Museum at the Villa Giulia, visitors have a unique opportunity to learn more about this intriguing people, whose complex civilization continues to astonish the world.

THIS MAGNIFICENT BAS-RELIEF
IS FROM THE SANCTUARY DEDICATED TO THE WHITE GODDESS OF THE SEA,
WHOM THE GREEKS CALLED LEUCOTEA.
THE FIGURES ILLUSTRATE THE TRAGIC EPISODE "SEVEN AGAINST THEBES,"
AS ZEUS HURLS A THUNDERBOLT AT THE HERO CAMPANEUS,
WHILE TIDEUS SEIZES THE HEAD OF THE THEBAN MELANIPPUS WITH HIS TEETH,
BENEATH ATHENA'S HORRIFIED GAZE.

Museo dell' Olio Della Sabina

The Sabine Olive Oil Museum

Viale Regina Margherita, N. 21
Castelnuovo di Farfa
Rieti 02031
Tel: 07/653–6370

Open Tuesday through Sunday
10:00 A.M. to 2:00 P.M. and
5:00 P.M. to 8:00 P.M.
April to September;
10:00 A.M. to 1:00 P.M. and
3:00 P.M. to 6:00 P.M.
October and November;
11:00 A.M. to 4:00 P.M.
December to March.
**Closed Monday, Christmas Eve,
Christmas Day, December 31,
and January 1.**
Pre-arranged guided tours
are available for groups.
Disabled access, free parking.

**By metro: Take the Fiumicino
Airport-Orte line to Fara Sabina,
then a taxi (fifteen-minute ride)
to the museum. Groups can
pre-arrange transportation from
Fara Sabina to the museum.
By car: Take the SS. Salaria in
the direction of Rieti, leave
the Salaria at the 53rd km—
Osteria Nuova—and take the SP.
Mirtense, then follow the
signs for Castelnuovo di Farfa.**

ABOUT forty kilometers east of
Rome lies the Sabina region, whose
landscape of rolling, olive-tree
covered foothills and steep, forested
mountainsides, dotted with Medieval
hill towns, fortresses, and monaster-
ies, has remained unchanged for centuries. Olive trees have been cultivated
for thousands of years in Sabina—in
fact, archaeological finds confirm that
olives were already being harvested
during the sixth and seventh centuries
B.C. Sabina's mild climate and southern exposure offer the ideal condi-
tions for olive cultivation, although its
hilly landscape makes mechanized
agriculture impractical. Because most
of the olive groves have remained
family-owned properties, the olives
are still harvested by hand.

Sabine olive oil was the first in
Italy to receive the 'D.O.C.' grade of
quality. (As with fine wines, this
means the oil conforms to certain
quality and taste standards.) Apparently
these standards have been maintained
for centuries: the Greek physician
Galen (A.D. 129–c. 199) considered
Sabina's olive oil to be the finest in
the ancient world, and recommended
it for pharmaceutical preparations, as
well as for cooking.

While most of us view olive oil as
a delicious and healthy addition to
our diet, the ancient Romans seemed
to have spent much of their lives
anointing themselves with olive oil.
They oiled after the bath, before (and
sometimes during) meals, before and
after physical exercise, and whenever
they felt the need to relieve tension
and fatigue.

Today, the Sabine Olive Oil
Museum, in recognition of the

region's enduring association with one of earth's most fundamental foods, aims to reinterpret the significance of olive tree cultivation and the usage of olive oil. Created by the architects Mao Benedetti and Sveva Di Martino, the museum is in the handsomely restored fourteenth-century Palazzo Perelli in the center of Castelnuova di Farfa, a hillside town near the monumental and cele-brated Farfa Abbey, one of the most important religious centers during the Middle Ages. (It was this very abbey which maintained the cultivation and exploitation of the olive tree at a time when it was in general decline.)

"Our challenge in Italy is to find a special and personal way to show the world the cultural richness and variety of our country, and illuminate the myths in our history," explains Di Martino. "What could be more legendary than the myth of a primor-dial bitter fruit—the olive—that somebody realized could be trans-formed into one of the 'sweet' foods of the world? How is this different from the metaphor of art, which transforms inert matter into culture?"

A CEMENT WALL CONCEIVED BY
ARTIST MARIA LAI,
CHISELED WITH WORDS AND PHRASES
LINKED TO ART AND OLIVE OIL,
INTRODUCES VISITORS TO THE MUSEUM'S
CONTEMPORARY ART SECTION.

OLEOFONA, A MUSICAL INSTALLATION CREATED BY GIANANDREA GAZZOLA,
IS DEPENDENT UPON OLIVE OIL DRIPPING INTO THESE EIGHTEENTH-CENTURY
TERRA-COTTA OIL JUGS, WHICH ARE EMBEDDED IN THE PERELLI PALACE'S WALLS.

Seeing themselves as "miners of Italy's living past," both architects have chosen to use ancient rural tools such as an eighteenth-century millstone for crushing olives and fragments from a wooden olive press, as well as didactic texts and vivid illustrations, to present the time-honored process of making olive oil. A wall of fine black-and-white photographs and transcribed interviews with local farmers, presents a panorama that highlights the challenging aspects of olive cultivation and processing—an enlightening component for visitors who have had limited exposure to rural life.

Yet, what makes this museum truly notable is the directors' decision to commission contemporary artists to create provocative works that pay visual, sensual, and even sonic tribute to olive oil.

Traveling Olive Tree, by the Japanese artist Hidetoshi Nagasawa (born 1940), located in the museum's lower level, consists of a suspended upside-down boat of brass tubing from which hangs an upside-down copper "olive tree" covered with over a thousand leaves in copper. Beneath the tree is a water-filled basin, illuminated by a small fleet of oil-filled copper boats. "Nagasawa celebrates the olive tree, which comes to us in a symbolic boat from a mystical dimension where East and West converge, and where water can also become sky, since the oil lamps can seem like stars," notes Di Martino.

Even more unusual is *Oleofona (Oleophone),* a sculpture conceived by

Gianandrea Gazzola (born 1948), that uses olive oil to make music. His installation, which takes up two adjoining rooms, uses four glass oil droppers to make music. The music's pitch is set by the level of the oil at the very points where each drop falls; the timbre evolves from natural sound to more complex waves. In the next room, electronic sensors attached to a big olive tree trunk, which slowly rotates upon itself, help to shape the music's sounds.

After contemplating such atypical works of art, visitors can learn more about the olive, thanks to informative texts in both Italian and English that describe the transformation of this legendary fruit from bushy plant to prized, fragrant oil. The olive is the only fruit with a high fat content: its precious store of oil—seventeen percent of the fruit's substance—is contained in pockets within the fruit's cells. No wonder the word *oil* comes

from *oliva*, the Latin word for olive.

This fine liquid, it turns out, comes from a fruit which, in its pristine state, picked straight from the tree, tastes *horrible*. When the oil in the olive flesh is pressed out, an extremely bitter substance, called *oleuropein*, is siphoned off with the vegetable water. Difficult to dispose of, it may become a dangerous pollutant. The ancient Romans used to call this residue *amurca*, and used it as a weed-killer and insecticide.

In order to become edible, olives must be soaked in lye and carefully washed, then cured in brine. However, even before the fruit is harvested, the olive trees must be subjected to a rigorous scientific process of grafting, pruning, and protection from the elements.

Olive trees can live for centuries, sending deep taproots down into the soil in search of water. If a tree is cut down or burned, the root survives and can spontaneously send out fresh suckers from its base underground. For this reason, the olive tree has represented ideas of regeneration and immortality: green shoots miraculously growing out of a charred stump. The shoots of a plant are called *scions*—a word that has also come to mean human offspring.

This ability to begin again is also linked to the tree's extreme longevity. (Local tradition maintains that in Canneto—a small town in Sabina—there is the largest olive tree in Europe, whose trunk measures over seven meters in circumference, and whose estimated age exceeds two thousand years.)

For the finest olive oil, the fruit must be picked individually, by hand. The olive harvest of Sabina has always been regarded as one of the high points of the year, comparable with the grape harvest elsewhere. It is a social event, complete with picnics and a tasting of the famous *bruschetta* (toasted bread rubbed with garlic and anointed with the new oil), when the quality of the oil can finally be appreciated. This tradition is still maintained each year on the third Sunday of October in Castelnuova di Farfa, at "the Feast of Oil Milling." To help visitors appreciate this local custom, the museum provides several mouth-watering recipes explaining the preparation of *bruschetta*.

Artist Maria Lai's (born 1919) conceptual work, using the palace's ancient bakery as a backdrop, also pays homage to this time-honored tradition. Titled *Olio al pane alla terra il sogno (Oil to Bread and to Earth the Dream)*, the piece is intended to highlight the marriage of the just-milled oil and freshly-baked bread, products of the earth, as well as of the human imagination. The palace's old wood-burning oven is filled with thirty pieces of white

THIS ANCIENT BAKERY WAS RECLAIMED BY ARTIST MARIA LAI FOR HER INSTALLATION *OIL TO BREAD AND TO EARTH THE DREAM.*

THIS MODERN STEEL-AND-GLASS STRUCTURE RE-CREATES THE ANCIENT APSE
OF THE SAN DONATO CHURCH, NEXT TO THE PERELLI PALACE.

ceramic "loaves" that are in the midst of rising. Other "breads" in brown ceramic are presented on a wood board, next to a white ceramic oil cruet, intended for oiling the bread. Each ceramic "loaf" has the imprint of an olive branch, illustrating the time-honored bond between bread and olive oil.

"In this museum, we are trying to show that contemporary art can co-exist with an ancient olive mill, that a modern documentation center can be in harmony with a historical palace and the surrounding Medieval town," says Di Martino. "Today, Italian museums can no longer only preserve and collect historical things, but must become places where the past can speak through modern media, including contemporary art." Certainly, the Sabine Olive Oil Museum offers a stimulating display in words and images that demonstrates how one of the world's most ancient and vital plants can still bear new and intriguing cultural fruits.

Museo dello Sbarco di Anzio
The Anzio Beachhead Museum

Villa Adele
Via degli Elci
Anzio 00042
Tel: 06/984-5147

Open Tuesday, Thursday,
Saturday, Sunday
Summer: 10:00 A.M. to 12:30 P.M.
and 5:00 P.M. to 7:00 P.M.
Winter: 10:00 A.M. to 12:30 P.M.
and 4:00 P.M. to 6:00 P.M.

By train: Take the train to
Anzio from the Termini Station
in Rome, then walk two minutes
to Via degli Elci, following the
signs to the museum.
By car: From Via Pontina,
take ss 201 to Via Nettunense,
then take the exit for Anzio.

FLANKING THE MUSEUM'S ENTRANCE
ARE A PROPELLER FROM A FIAT PLANE
THAT WAS DOWNED OVER ANZIO,
AND THE ANCHOR FROM A BOAT
THAT PARTICIPATED IN THE
AMERICAN LANDING AT ANZIO.

ALFREDO Rinaldi can remember hearing the announcement of the Allied landing at Anzio on January 22, 1944, as if it were yesterday. "I was in Rome, and I heard it on Italian radio at 2:25 A.M. I was so excited, because I knew that it meant the war would soon be over."

More than a half-century after the five-month-long battle that led to the liberation of Rome, Rinaldi presides over what he regards as the greatest accomplishment of his life, the Anzio Beachhead Museum, inaugurated exactly fifty years to the day that he first heard of the Allied invasion.

Housed on the ground floor of the Villa Adele—the first summer residence built by a cardinal in Anzio around 1620—the one-room museum is crowded with weapons and uniforms from British, American, Commonwealth, German, and Italian forces, together with battle plans and maps, flags and ensigns, propaganda posters and leaflets, assorted medals, insignias, photos, and newspaper clippings—all paying tribute to the men who fought and often died at Anzio. Many exhibits, including a German military motorcycle, the remains of airplanes, landing craft, and warships, have been retrieved from the seabed in Anzio's port.

In fact, a number of sunken ships with remains of their crew still aboard lie in the depths of the Tyrrhenian Sea, including the H.M.S. *Spartan,* the H.M.S. *Janus,* and the U.S. Hospital Ship *St. David.* (Most of the exhibits on display have been either generously donated by veterans and their families or purchased through private donations.)

THE WARTIME MEMORABILIA SHOWN HERE INCLUDES
AN OVERCOAT WORN BY AN ENGLISH SOLDIER, AN AMERICAN-MADE MACHINE-GUN,
A TWO-WAY CANADIAN RADIO,
AND A SEARCHLIGHT PROJECTOR MADE BY GENERAL ELECTRIC
THAT WAS RECOVERED FROM THE DEPTHS OF THE COVE INSIDE THE PORT OF ANZIO.

If this modest museum has a special significance for Rinaldi, it is certainly understandable. At sixteen, three months after the Allied landing, armed only with the rashness of youth, he stole away in the middle of the night, and headed for Anzio to see whether his family's home was still standing. While the German lines around the beachhead were strong enough to hem in the Allies, this underfed Italian adolescent was able to pass through them without any harm. Rinaldi believes that, if the Germans had seen him but didn't shoot, it was because they were afraid to give away their own positions.

However, near Aprilia, he met his

first American soldiers, who did what the Germans had not attempted to do—they arrested him! When finally convinced of his innocence, his captors released him and he made his way into Anzio. Here he was "adopted" by the soldiers of the 58th Company of the Fifth Army's U.S. 85th Division Quartermasters. Captain Kirby, Lieutenant Brooks, and Sergeant Fran White became his "guardian angels"— he was to spend much of the remainder of the war carrying out all sorts of tasks for them until the 85th Division finally reached Camp Darby in Livorno. During this period, he rode through Rome in an Army truck and was hailed as a liberator alongside his new-found American friends.

While the passing of time and fifty years of peace in Western Europe permit Rinaldi to recall with nostalgia his days as a mascot with the 85th Division, the museum's documentation mainly underscores the chaos, carnage, and courage of war, all of

which were in ample supply during the long, drawn-out campaign at Anzio.

Under the code name "Operation Shingle," a January 1944 Allied landing at Anzio had been strenuously advocated by Britain's Prime Minister Winston Churchill and approved by the Allies at the Marrakech Conference earlier that same month. The orders, albeit vague, given to General John P. Lucas, commander of the Sixth U.S. Corps which disembarked at Anzio, were to establish a solid beachhead near Anzio, and then cut the enemy's main lines of communication by occupying the Alban Hills and taking the XIV German Army Corps at the rear, with the ultimate aim of penetrating the heavily fortified Gustav Line.

Much to the Allies' astonishment, the initial landing at Anzio was virtually unopposed, as the Germans had suspended a 24-hour coastal watch. By the evening of January 23, the 1st British Division had occupied

THIS 1945 PHOTO WAS TAKEN OF
ALFREDO RINALDI POSING PROUDLY IN AN AMERICAN JEEP.

ABOVE THE GLASS SHOWCASE FILLED WITH WARTIME SOUVENIRS
ARE PHOTOS OF AUDIE MURPHY AND HIS MANY MEDALS.
MURPHY WAS THE MOST DECORATED AMERICAN SOLDIER IN WORLD WAR II.

the left side of the port, while the
3rd U.S. Division had taken the right.
Yet, this golden moment of surprise
was to prove short-lived. Within days,
the Germans had succeeded in bring-
ing in substantial reinforcements from
as· far away as Yugoslavia, so that by
the end of January the Allied advance
had been halted and they had suffered
over 3,000 casualties.

(The heavy toll in Allied forces is
confirmed in the two cemeteries in
Nettuno, and the one at Cassino,
the largest in Italy. To this day, many
military historians contend that
the invading forces could have spared
many lives, had they *immediately*
pressed on toward Rome after
discovering there were practically no
German combat troops in the area.)

Over the next four months,
the battle of Anzio turned into static
warfare, with the Allied troops virtually living in the trenches, sometimes

ALFREDO RINALDI SITS ON A GERMAN BMW MOTORCYCLE
THAT WAS FOUND IN THE VICINITY OF ANZIO IN 1944, AND WHICH STILL FUNCTIONS TODAY.

uncovering Roman ruins in the process. "After the war, the British and American soldiers told me that they were so close to the enemy in the field, that they would call to each other asking for cigarettes at night," Rinaldi recalls with feeling. "The next day, they would start fighting all over again. Imagine, fighting against men with whom you had shared cigarettes only a few hours earlier."

After a long period of stalemate, and a regrouping of the Allied forces, the final attack on the Gustav Line began on May 11 and 12, this time catching the Germans off-guard as they were in the midst of reorganizing their forces. Yet, it wasn't until a bold assault by French troops fighting under the U.S. Fifth Army in mid-May that the Allies were able to successfully pierce the Gustav Line and force the enemy to retreat. Two weeks after this successful battle on June 4, 1944, the first Allied troops entered Rome.

While the strategic importance of the Battle of Anzio in the liberation of Italy has been well-documented, the campaign's contribution to the overall Allied endeavor in Europe has often been underestimated. The two German corps engaged on the Anzio front were originally destined for the beaches of Normandy. Historians now believe that the success of the landings off the coast of France in June 1944 was due, in part, to the tenacity and courage of the Allied forces at Anzio.

Yet the price of this crucial victory was high. The Allies suffered nearly 28,000 casualties. As a measure of the courage and sacrifice of those who fought at Anzio, twenty-two Americans were awarded the Congressional Medal of Honor, the most of any single battle in World War II.

Every year, on Memorial Day, Rinaldi visits the American Cemetery in Nettuno where some eight thousand soldiers are buried. In 1989, during a visit by President George Bush, he met a correspondant from *The Stars and Stripes* newspaper, who went on to publish Rinaldi's wartime story. Read by veterans of the 85th Quartermaster Depot Supply Company, Alfredo was invited to

the United States for their annual reunion. After almost fifty years, Rinaldi was able to embrace his "guardian angels" once more, and with their assistance, gathered many of the wartime artifacts and memorabilia that are now on display in the museum.

"I cannot forget what they did for us," he says, tears welling up in his eyes. "I remember them looking for civilians left on the battlefield so they could give them some food.

"One American soldier helped deliver a baby from Anzio on an American man-of-war that was evacuating wartime refugees from Anzio to Naples," he continues, pointing to a faded newspaper clipping. "That 'baby' now works in the Palmolive factory at Anzio. I keep it all fresh in my mind—everything that they did for Italy."

Today, Rinaldi feels he has both the obligation and the pleasure of transmitting his experiences and knowledge to a younger generation of visitors who have been spared the horrors of war. Jennifer Browne, the daughter of one American veteran who fought at Anzio, wrote to Rinaldi after visiting the Anzio Beachhead Museum: "All the facts, figures, and strategies became faces, names, and personal tragedies. The museum forces one to realize the true essence of war.

"Many soldiers died in this battle and that is a horrible fact. For other soldiers, their battle began after the war, in attempting to rebuild their lives knowing such devastating experiences had occurred. Alfredo is the guardian angel of the veteran. He guides and protects the memories of Anzio."

The National Roman Museum in the Palazzo Altemps

Piazza di S. Apollinare, N. 46–48
Rome 00186
Tel: 06/322–6571

**Open Tuesday through Saturday
9:00 A.M. to 7:00 P.M.
Open Sunday 9:00 A.M. to
2:00 P.M.**

Bus: 60, 64, 70, 81, 94

AT THE SUMMIT OF
THE ROOFTOP LOGGIA OF
PALAZZO ALTEMPS IS THE HERALDIC IBEX
OF ROBERTO ALTEMPS.
ERECTED AT THE END OF THE
SIXTEENTH CENTURY
BY CARDINAL MARCO SITTICO ALTEMPS.
THE PALACE WAS INTENDED TO
HONOR THE MEMORY OF
HIS SON ROBERTO, WHO WAS CONDEMNED
TO DEATH FOR ADULTERY IN 1586
BY POPE SIXTUS V.

APPROACHING the unassuming façade of Palazzo Altemps, which is a five-minute walk from the Piazza Navona, it is difficult to imagine that this stolid stone edifice was once the site of a grand celebration of the birth of the French Dauphin to Louis XV and Marie Leszczynska in 1754—an extravaganza that rivaled those which had been mounted when the Holy Roman Emperor Charles V visited Rome two centuries earlier.

On this occasion, Cardinal Melchior de Polignac, Ambassador to the Court of France, invited three thousand guests to the palace to see an opera that had been specifically composed to acclaim the royal heir. Not only did the Cardinal provide his guests with abundant refreshments and costly delicacies, he also ordered that the fountain in the middle of the piazza opposite the palace should continuously gush wine.

While such spectacular festivities are impossible to replicate today, visitors to the Palazzo Altemps are bound to concur that its painstaking restoration and the handsome installation of one of the world's most notable ancient sculpture collections, are also cause for celebration. "The Palazzo Altemps provides space suitable for the display of sculpture and statuary that have been hidden for too long," maintains Dott.ssa Matilde De Angelis d'Ossat, director of the museum's collection of ancient sculpture. "Having waited several centuries, we have finally achieved the rehabilitation and restitution of part of an historic heritage which had been removed from the public domain," she adds.

THE CUPBOARD ROOM FEATURES THE FAMOUS GREEK MARBLE STATUE OF *ARES* or *MARS*,
WHICH WAS PARTLY RESTORED BY GIAN LORENZO BERNINI IN 1622.

Located in an area that in ancient times was occupied by marble workshops, most probably in the vicinity of a temple dedicated to Apollo, the construction of Palazzo Altemps was undertaken during several intervals, beginning in the latter part of the fifteenth century. Work on the palace continued under Cardinal Francesco Soderini from Volterra between 1511 and 1523, and was finally completed by the Austrian Cardinal Marco Sittico Altemps and his heirs after 1568.

A tour of the thick-walled palace will help one to understand why some visitors consider the Palazzo Altemps a museum within a museum. Fragments of frescoes (uncovered during the building's latest restoration) hint at the palace's previously lavish decoration, and confirm the mastery of even minor artists in the field of landscape and still-life painting during the Renaissance.

The Painted Views Room features a charming wooded landscape at sunset, a hunting scene, and a broad view with an obelisk, while the Cupboard Room depicts an impressive sideboard laden with silver-and-gold wedding plate and piles of greeting cards, commemorating the 1477 marriage of Girolamo Riario and Caterina Sforza. (They were the first residents of Palazzo Altemps.)

Yet it is the palace's painted loggia, commissioned by Marco Sittico Altemps, that demonstrates a particular taste for the opulent and the exotic. Painted to resemble a secret garden of delights, the loggia's vaulting reveals not only an extremely refined *trompe-l'oeil* technique, but also an interest in the animals and fruits that had been discovered on expeditions to the New World.

After a part of the palace collapsed in 1575, it was reinforced, and subsequently enlarged and redecorated to accommodate Cardinal Altemps's two outstanding collections: the Altemps Library (now part of the Vatican Library), and a remarkable group of ancient statuary, that was cited in Roman guidebooks published in the seventeenth and eighteenth centuries.

However, as a result of the family's dwindling fortunes, by the end of the eighteenth century much of the statuary had been sold during a period of intense traffic in antiquities, and only sixteen of the one hundred statues that once made up the famed collection are in the palazzo today. The sculptures that were sold now figure among the prize holdings of the Vatican Museum, the British Museum, the Louvre, the Pushkin Museum, and the Hermitage, as well as museums in Berlin and Copenhagen.

Despite these losses, the Palazzo Altemps still contains an embarrassment of riches. In addition to the sculptures remaining from the original collection, the museum also boasts works from the Ludovisi Boncompagni Collection and the

THIS VAST ROOM, KNOWN AS THE FIREPLACE SALON, WAS ONCE USED AS A PICTURE GALLERY
AND AS THE SETTING FOR FESTIVE GATHERINGS.
IN THE CENTER OF THE ROOM IS THE *GALATIAN SUICIDE AND HIS SPOUSE,*
AN ANCIENT MARBLE COPY OF THE PERGAMON BRONZE.

THIS PAINTED LOGGIA, WITH ITS *TROMPE-L'OEIL* "GARDEN OF DELIGHTS,"
DISPLAYS THE SO-CALLED TWELVE CAESARS FROM THE LUDOVISI COLLECTION.

Mattei Collection, as well as Egyptian sculptures from the National Roman Museum, and other minor collections.

Among the Palazzo Altemps's prize sculptures are works from the Boncompagni Ludovisi Collection, begun by the Bolognese Cardinal Ludovico Ludovisi, nephew of Pope Gregory XV, who reigned from 1621 to 1623. Enriched by his uncle's papal election, Cardinal Ludovisi built a magnificent villa on the Quirinal Hill (the highest in Rome), and decorated it with paintings and a collection of ancient statuary acquired from other prominent Roman families, or from excavations made in the garden during the villa's construction. (Such surrendipitous finds were made possible, partly because the Cardinal's villa was built on the grounds of Julius Caesar's summer palace and gardens, later acquired by Sallust, the wealthy Roman historian.)

Established Baroque sculptors, such as Lorenzo Bernini and Alessandro Algardi, were engaged by Cardinal Ludovisi to restore and even polish these sculptures, something that would be considered unthinkable today. Adorned with this exceptional ancient statuary, Cardinal Ludovisi's garden became an obligatory place for artists and tourists to visit during their stay in Rome.

Not only did a number of visitors request permission from the Ludovisi family to make molds of these ancient statues, but the eighteenth-century German archaeologist Johann Joachim Winckelmann studied these sculptures when he was compiling his history of ancient art.

By the nineteenth century, the Ludovisi estate extended over 74 acres and boasted a collection of 339 sculptures. However, in 1883, Prince Rodolfo Boncompagni Ludovisi sold the property to developers, much to the dismay of the international cultural community. While unable to prevent the garden's destruction so that a new urban district could be built (it is now the site of the American Embassy), 104 works from the collection were purchased by the Italian government in 1901.

Given the evidence that the Altemps and the Ludovisi families had bought and sold statues from each other's collections over the centuries, the museum's directors were persuaded that the Palazzo Altemps would be a fitting home for Cardinal Ludovisi's former collection of ancient sculptures.

Among the most stunning works on display are a handsome god-like soldier, the *Ludovisi Mars* or *Ares,* a Roman copy of an original from the Hellenistic age, restored in 1622 by Gian Lorenzo Bernini; a lively version of *Electra and Her Brother Orestes,* a work from the first century A.D. by Menelaus, an artist of the school of Praxiteles; and an idealized *Apollo with Lyre* (his head was inspired by the Vatican's *Apollo Belvedere*).

Perhaps one of the most gripping works in the museum is the *Galatian Suicide and His Spouse,* discovered in the seventeenth century on the property once owned by Julius Caesar and Sallust. This affecting sculpture, commissioned by Julius Caesar to celebrate his victory over the Gauls, was modeled after a group of bronzes first made for the King of Pergamon, Attalus I, to commemorate his victory over the Galatians. (Galatia, an ancient territory in central Asia Minor, now near Ankara, in Turkey, was successively conquered by the Gauls, the Greeks, and the Romans.)

Another treasure—that would be difficult to overlook—is the colossal head of the *Ludovisi Hera* or *Juno,* at least three times life-size. Winckelmann believed that no statue better represented the classical canons of thoughtfulness and Olympian serenity. Its greatest admirer was Goethe, who immortalized the work in his *Italian Journey* and had a plaster cast made of the sculpture, which he later gave to the painter Angelica Kaufmann. Recently, scholars have identified the majestic head as an idealized portrait of Antonia Augusta, the mother of the Emperor Claudius, who was deified after her death and extolled by her son as an unsurpassed example of marital fidelity and maternal devotion.

The most famous work in the museum, discovered in 1887 during the urbanization of the Villa Ludovisi, has come to be known as the Ludovisi "throne," a fifth-century B.C. Greek marble altarpiece brought to Rome after the conquest of Greece. Believed to have been a throne used in theatrical liturgies honoring the Goddess of Love, it had originally been kept in the Aphrodite sanctuary at Locri Epizefiri, on the Ionic coast of Calabria. The throne's principal bas-relief decoration depicts Aphrodite being supported by two handmaidens as she is born from the surf of the sea; on the left side is a nude female flutist seated on a cushion, on the right, a cloaked woman making an incense offering (possibly two priestesses of the cult of Aphrodite).

DECORATED WITH FRESCOES FROM THE STORY OF MOSES,
THIS GALLERY CONTAINS THE MONUMENTAL LUDOVISI THRONE PORTRAYING
THE BIRTH OF APHRODITE.
ON THE LEFT SIDE OF THE THRONE, A NUDE FEMALE FIGURE PLAYS THE FLUTE.

Describing the spellbinding beauty of Aphrodite in this bas-relief, Georgina Masson wrote in *The Companion Guide to Rome:* "All the joy and surprise of life are mirrored in her upturned face, as smiling she stretches up her arms to the two nymphs who raise her out of the depths on to the pebbled shore. It is a thing unique, never to be forgotten; and to the writer at any rate the most beautiful sculpture in Rome." To be able to partake in an aesthetic experience of this magnitude seems reason enough to visit the beautifully restored and treasure-filled Palazzo Altemps.

Palazzo Farnese a Caprarola

The Palazzo Farnese at Caprarola

Viterbo 01032
Tel: 0761/646–052

Open Monday through Saturday
9:00 A.M. to 4:00 P.M.
November through February;
9:00 A.M. to 5:00 P.M. in March;
9:00 A.M. to 6:00 P.M.
April, May, and September;
9:00 A.M. to 7:00 P.M.
June through August.

By bus: Cottral from Rome's
Saxa Rubra to Viterbo.
By car: Coming from Rome, take
route SS/2 Cassia, direction to
Monterosi or from the freeway
A/1 Exit at Orte, then take
the route to Viterbo, and then
Caprarola.

ALTHOUGH not as well-known as the Renaissance châteaux of the Loire Valley, the palatial villas of Latium can be just as breathtaking— combining architectural innovation with elaborate gardens bedecked with statuary and fountains. Such a villa is the Palazzo Farnese at Caprarola, seventy kilometers north of Rome, considered to be the finest edifice ever built by the architect Giacomo Barozzi da Vignola (1507–1573). (Vignola, who succeeded Michelangelo as architect in charge of St. Peter's, is also remembered for his design of the church Il Gesù in Rome, and his treatise on the five orders of architecture, based upon the work of the Roman architect, engineer, and

THE PLEASURE CASINO AND FOUNTAINS AT CAPRAROLA:
THE BUILDING OF THIS ELEGANT EDIFICE WAS THE FINAL PHASE
OF AN ENORMOUS PROJECT.
THE ARCHITECT APPEARS TO HAVE BEEN JACOPO DEL DUCA,
WHO ALSO CREATED THE GARDENS AND FOUNTAINS SURROUNDING THE FARNESE PALACE.

author Vitruvius, an essay that has been adhered to as an almost inviolable authority.)

If the Roman aesthete Mario Praz declared Caprarola the "bible of the rich" and compared it with the splendors of Chartres Cathedral, it is not surprising. Caprarola was built and decorated to exalt the glory of its owner, Cardinal Alessandro Farnese (1520–1589), the nephew of Pope Paul III.

When Alessandro was appointed Cardinal on the election of his uncle to the Holy See, he was submerged overnight by a wealth of bishoprics, honors, and titles. Not only did he travel as a papal envoy to Avignon and Germany, but he also played an important role in the elections of successive popes, as well as in the deliberations of the 1545 Council of Trent, convened to impose Church reforms. Greatly admired by the Holy Roman Emperor Charles V for his virtue and sagacity, Farnese was a shrewd diplomat and a demanding taskmaster, known for his love of art, science, and literature. He is remembered for saying that "there is nothing more despicable than a cowardly soldier or an ignorant priest."

At the beginning of the sixteenth century, the Farnese family bought the small estate of Caprarola, which the Cardinal chose as his summer residence, a move that was to alter the character of the little village. At the Cardinal's behest, Vignola built a raised street on the same axis as the palace, demolished old houses and built new ones in their place, creating in the process a small masterpiece in urbanization that exists in Caprarola to this day.

Although the original structure of the Farnese palace had been designed in the 1520s by Baldassare Peruzzi and Antonio da Sangallo the Younger as a two-story fortress with bulwarks, ramparts, moat, and drawbridges (prepared to withstand any marauding forces), this type of edifice was no longer appropriate to the needs of a Renaissance court.

Vignola's disposition of the palace at Caprarola was coherent with the ideals of its owner: it was intended not only to represent the power of a new feudal family, but also to serve as a unique country estate for an important ambassador of the Faith. Positioned on the top of a hill, the pentagonal palace dominates the town, which seems to huddle around its base. Nor is there any doubt where the town leaves off and the villa begins. Visitors have to climb a double set of circular stairs and cross open forecourts to reach the villa's main entrance. In approaching the monumental façade, visitors may feel a fleeting twinge of insignificance. (As an interesting footnote, the Dayton Art Institute in Dayton, Ohio, built on a hilltop overlooking the city's downtown, was modeled after the Palazzo Farnese at Caprarola.)

The four-story palace is notable for its lavish interior painted decoration attributed to the leading Mannerist artists of the period, including Taddeo and Frederico Zuccari, Giacomo Bertoja, Giovanni de Vecchi, Raffaellino da Reggio, and Antonio Tempesta. Although Cardinal Farnese inspired the palace's embellishments, he relied on the poet Annibal Caro, as well as his relatives Onofrio Panvinio and Fulvio Orsini, to elaborate its dazzling iconography—a synthesis of mythology, biblical epics, family history, culture, and science, all converging to glorify this Roman dynasty. (Because the execution of this complex decorative scheme was fraught with difficulties, the palace, which was begun in 1555, was only completed in 1583.)

Inside, it requires a sustained effort

THE FRESCOES IN THE ROOM
OF THE FARNESE SPLENDORS WERE EXECUTED
CHIEFLY BY
FEDERICO AND TADDEO ZUCCARI,
AS WELL AS BY GIOVANNI ANTINORO.

not to be overwhelmed by the staggering volumes and frescoes, starting with the monumental circular courtyard and adjacent portico, whose barrel vault is decorated with a pergola, rich in greenery, flowers, and birds against a pale blue sky. Right above it, on the *piano nobile,* is an equally magnificent loggia leading into the Farnese state apartments.

(Hidden from view are two additional floors, one for the Cavaliers, the other for the Grooms, each one containing sixty-one rooms.)

Those who paid the Cardinal a visit must have been as awed as visitors are today by the magnificent helicoidal staircase, connecting the underground floor to the *piano nobile.* Regarded as Vignola's

THESE FRESCOES IN THE ROOM OF THE COUNCIL OF TRENT WERE THE WORK OF
THE ZUCCARI BROTHERS, WHILE THE *TROMPE-L'OEIL* COLUMNS WERE DONE BY VIGNOLA.
IF SOMEONE STANDS IN A CORNER OF THIS ROOM
HE OR SHE CAN HEAR SOMEONE ELSE WHISPER AT THE OPPOSITE END OF THE ROOM,
AS IF THAT PERSON WERE STANDING RIGHT NEXT TO THEM.

masterpiece, it was inspired by Bramante's stairs in the Vatican. Supported by thirty Doric, Ionian, and Corinthian paired columns, which correspond to an identical number of facing pillars carved out of the same stone, the spiral staircase is embellished with balustrades, niches, and the Farnese coat of arms, and lavishly decorated with grotesques, allegorical figures, and landscapes by Antonio Tempesta and his assistants.

This showpiece was intended to prepare visitors for the the overwhelming spectacle of the rooms on the mezzanine and the *piano nobile*. The so-called "summer apartments" on the mezzanine, consisting of four rooms illustrating the different seasons, together with the splendid

Jupiter Room depicting the *Legend of Jupiter and the Goat Amalthea* (who nursed him as a child), were painted in homage to the palace's location. (In fact, the Italian word for goat, *capra*, is within the name "Caprarola").

By far the largest and most splendid room in the summer quarters is the Jupiter Room, first decorated by Taddeo Zuccari (1560–61). It is hard to know which is more dazzling— the exquisitely painted scenes and grotesques on the ceiling illustrating the myth of Jupiter who transforms the goat into a constellation, or the walls decorated with a series of perspective paintings of illusory columns, atriums, statues, and landscapes attributed to Vignola, all of which conspire to make the already grandiose space appear even larger than it is.

The religious yet worldly personality of Cardinal Farnese is revealed in the totality of the palace's transformation and decorative scheme. Oblivious of any existing harsh reality beyond the painted walls, the paintings are intended to associate mythological figures with family enterprises and history. Nowhere is this more opulently expressed than in the room of the Farnese Splendors *(Fasti Farnesini)*, whose dimensions correspond to the Jupiter Room on the floor below.

These scenes, which must have influenced the decorations of the Hall of Mirrors at Versailles illustrating the exploits of Louis XIV, were painted to demonstrate that the Farnese had always played a leading role in Italian life and had always triumphed over their enemies. The ceiling's two tondos and four squares recall how Guido Farnese quelled the Viterbo uprisings in 1323, how Pietro Nicolo Farnese liberated Bologna in 1361, how another Pietro Farnese, after the defeat of Pisa, triumphantly entered Florence in 1362, and finally how Ranuccio, grandfather of Pope Paul III, was appointed captain of the Church by Eugene IV in 1435.

Both in the room illustrating the Farnese Splendors and in the Antechamber of the Council, the figure of Pope Paul III highlights a biography replete with historical events. Raised to the highest level of dignity, he is alternately shown wearing the papal crown, extending his foot to be kissed by the Emperor Charles V, excommunicating rebels like Henry VIII, elevating to cardinal famous men who would someday succeed him, and calling for the famous Council of Trent, the Catholic response to the Protestant Reformation.

When Taddeo Zuccari and Annibale Caro died suddenly in 1566, Taddeo's brother Federico didn't waste any time in offering his services to Cardinal Farnese. Working in close collaboration with the Cardinal's relatives, Fulvio Orsini and Ottavio Panvinio, Federico executed the decoration for the winter apartments and the mezzanine's Guardroom, as well as for the Chapel, the Hercules Room, and the Ermatena Room, on the *piano nobile*.

Most art historians agree that the pinnacle of Federico's work was reached in the Chapel, whose elaborate vault duplicates the floor motif designed by Vignola. Every facet of the room is pleasing to the eye, from the finely painted ceiling tondos, to the large figures in the perspective niches, which illustrate stories from the Gospels, to the central *Pietà* that Federico copied from one of Taddeo's paintings. (Federico, wishing to pay homage to Vignola and his brother in the Chapel, portrayed the former as Saint James and the latter as Saint Thaddeus.)

THE MAP ROOM TAKES ITS NAME FROM THE MAP OF THE WORLD DEPICTED AT ONE END.
THE FRESCOES HAVE BEEN ATTRIBUTED TO
RAFFAELLINO DA REGGIO AND GIOVANNI DE' VECCHI.
THE MAPS WERE PAINTED BY GIOVANNI ANTONIO DA VARESE,
WHO ALSO WORKED ON THE VATICAN PALACE.
THE FANCIFUL ZODIAC, WHICH SEEMS TO FLOAT ON THE CEILING,
IS THE WORK OF AN UNKNOWN ARTIST.

While the extensive architectural and pictorial riches within this palatial estate may appear somewhat staggering to behold, an appreciation of the extraordinary compendium of talent that gave birth to this unique palatial estate more than compensates for any possible impression of aesthetic surfeit. We can be grateful that despite the upheavals in the papacy over the centuries, the splendors of the Palazzo Farnese have retained their original beauty, a beauty that has contributed to Italy's well-earned reputation as being one of the world's leading repositories of magnificent art.

Palazzo I Galleria Spada

The Spada Palace and Gallery

Via Capodiferro, N. 3
Rome 00186
Tel: 06/686/1158

**Open Tuesday through Saturday
9:00 A.M. to 7:00 P.M.
Open Sunday 9:00 A.M. to
1:00 P.M.
Guided tours of the Palazzo
Spada's Council of State
Apartments available on
Sunday only.**

Bus: 19, 306, 926

THIS ENTRANCE TO
THE PALAZZO SPADA WAS BUILT FOR
THE CAPODIFERRO FAMILY,
THE FIRST OCCUPANTS OF THE PALACE.

Five minutes' walk from the austere and majestic façade of the Palazzo Farnese, is a stucco palace extravagantly decorated with Hellenistic heroes, medallions, urns, and swags of flowers. It is known as the Palazzo Spada, and there is nothing else like it in Rome.

Built originally in 1540 for Cardinal Girolamo Capodiferro, a papal nuncio, who had lived for many years at the court of the French King Francis I, it was acquired in 1632 by the fabulously wealthy Cardinal Bernardino Spada (a protégé of Pope Urban VIII), whose descendants finally sold it to the Italian state in 1926.

A special guided tour makes it possible for visitors to see the palatial state apartments (now used by the Italian Supreme Court), which are a vivid illustration of the transition from the Renaissance to the Baroque. One of these is the spectacular Stucco Gallery *(Galleria degli Stucchi)*, with its life-size stucco nudes and cherubs framing the paintings that line the walls and vaulted ceiling. Attributed to the master *stuccatore* Giulio Mazzoni of Modena, it is more than likely that this decorative scheme was inspired by the celebrated Francis I Gallery at Fontainebleau, a gallery with which Capodiferro must have been quite familiar, thanks to his diplomatic posting.

The adjacent Throne Room—used until 1870 for visiting popes—contains the celebrated *Statue of Pompey*. At the time of its discovery in 1550 in the Via dei Lutari (the Street of the Lute-makers), the statue was presumed to have been in the hall of

THE PERSPECTIVE OF
THIS COLONNADE BY FRANCESCO BORROMINI
CONVEYS THE ILLUSION
OF BEING MUCH LONGER THAN IT REALLY IS.
THE STATUE, WHICH APPEARS TO BE LIFE-SIZE,
IS ACTUALLY LESS THAN THREE FEET TALL.

Pompey's theater, where the Senate met on the fatal Ides of March in 44 B.C. So firm was contemporary opinion that this was the actual statue at whose feet Julius Caesar had been murdered, that a battle for its possession was settled only through the intervention of Pope Julius III. After the Pope acquired the remarkable statue (noted for the red veins running through its marble legs), he presented it to Cardinal Capodiferro, who installed it in his palace.

The historical claims surrounding this statue were so convincing, that for twenty years, up until World War II, an elderly Frenchwoman appeared punctually on the Ides of March to lay a bunch of red carnations at its feet. (In all likelihood, the statue originally ornamented the barracks of the chariot-racing "Greens," formerly on the site of the Via dei Lutari, where the Cancelleria Palace stands today.)

Cardinal Spada, who was one of the most cultivated art patrons in Rome, also took a keen interest in astronomy, a pursuit that is illustrated in the *Galleria di Meridiana* (Meridian Gallery) painted by Domenichino's pupil, G. B. Ruggeri. This artist created the illusion of a celestial sphere projected onto the gallery's barrel vault, a *tour de force* that is best appreciated by standing next to the window in the middle of the gallery. Equipped with a good working knowledge of physics *and* Latin, visitors will be able to decipher a complex ceiling sundial, which indicates different times around the world, including in Rome and in Dublin.

Eight celebrated Hellenistic reliefs from the first century A.D., discovered in 1620 near the church of S. Agnese fuori le Mura on the Via Nomentana, decorate the walls of this gallery. The fact that they were found lying face downward and had been used as *pavement*, accounts for their excellent condition.

While the state apartments are dazzling to behold, Palazzo Spada's most celebrated architectural feature is the illusionistic colonnade designed by the Baroque architect Francesco Borromini (1599–1667). What appears to be a gallery of thirty meters in length, terminating in a courtyard adorned with a statue of a statuesque male nude is, in fact, a colonnade measuring nine meters and containing a statue less than three feet in height. By sandwiching the gallery's columns (which gradually decrease in height), between an upward sloping floor and a downward sloping ceiling, Borromini was able to achieve this masterful illusion.

The palace's four-room art gallery on the second floor is unique in Rome—not only is it the only small familial collection to have remained intact, it also is displayed in its original setting. Furnished with marble-topped gilded-wood consoles, antique Roman sculpture, and an eclectic compilation of sacred and secular art, the collection reflects the tastes and interests of a wealthy dilettante. Visiting these sunlit rooms with their time-worn, polished terra-cotta floors, one has the impression of being transported back to another epoch, a sensation which is further enhanced by the playing of recorded Baroque music.

Art historians believe the small but choice collection was amassed mainly by Cardinal Bernardino Spada when he was the papal legate to Pope Urban VIII in Bologna around 1630. In room I, two portraits by Bologna's leading painters, Guido Reni (1575–1642) and Guercino (1591–1666), portray Spada as handsome, erudite, and self-possessed. In the Reni painting, he is shown writing a letter

THIS PORTRAIT OF CARDINAL BERNARDINO SPADA
IS BY GUIDO RENI.
TWO ROMAN MARBLE BUSTS (C. FIRST CENTURY A.D.)
AND A NEOCLASSICAL PENDULUM CLOCK
BY RAFAELLE FIORELLI,
ARE DISPLAYED ON THE GILDED CONSOLE.

to the Pope, whereas the Guercino portrait depicts him holding an architectural blueprint for a fortress near Bologna, whose construction he had been appointed to oversee.

It is interesting that Spada commissioned portraits from these two artistic rivals—their emnity was such that Reni accused Guercino of stealing both his technique and his ideas. (In fact, close examination of these Baroque painters reveals that they were both influenced by the same artists—Ludovico Carracci and Michelangelo Caravaggio.)

Between 1636 and 1637, the Cardinal added a left wing to the palace, which includes the gallery's rooms II and III. The first of these rooms, a small *studiolo* (study), features many formal male portraits, including an unfinished portrait of a violinist from Titian's workshop, portraits of a nobleman, an astrologist, and a botanist by Bartolomeo Passerotti (1528–1592), and a portrait of the Archbishop of Zara by Domenico Tintoretto (1560–1635). Yet, the works that most catch the eye are paintings by two women, an androgynous and helmeted *Cleopatra* by Lavinia Fontana (1552–1614), and *Portrait of a Young Girl* by Sofonisba Anguissola (1530–1625).

Anguissola was the first Italian woman artist to win international fame, and she opened the way for later women painters, many of whom were the daughters of artists. Raised by a widowed nobleman who was determined that both his daughters and son should receive a broad, enlightened education, Sofonisba and her sister Elena studied painting with a local artist, Bernardino Campi, and conveyed their training to their sisters, who also became artists.

Their father also engaged the help of Michelangelo, who sent Sofonisba a drawing that she could then color. When Sofonisba's work came to the attention of the Spanish Duke of Alba, then governor of Milan, she was invited to the Spanish court as a painter and lady-in-waiting to the Queen, where she remained for ten years.

The Spada Gallery also boasts works by a famous father-daughter painting duo: Orazio Gentileschi's (1563–1639) *David with the Head of Goliath,* and Artemisia Gentileschi's (1597–1651) *Virgin Nursing the Christ Child* (a spiritual evocation of motherhood), and *Santa Cecilia,* the patron saint of music.

Room III, known as the *Galleria del Cardinale* (The Cardinal's Gallery), features a spectacular ceiling and decorative frieze made of tempera on canvas, depicting allegorical figures of "The Four Parts of the World"

(Europe, Asia, Africa and America), "The Four Elements" (Earth, Air, Fire and Water) and "The Four Seasons," which were painted by Michelangelo Ricciolini (1654–1715) and his assistants at the behest of Fabrizio Spada, a family descendant. Among the outstanding pictures in this room are Jan "Velvet" Brueghel's *Landscape with Windmills,* Rubens's portrait of *A Cardinal,* and Nicolo Tornioli's Caravaggesque *Cain Killing Abel.*

Also worth noting are the room's furnishings, including some late sixteenth-century stools in painted wood with reliefs in papier-mâché, decorated with the escutcheon of Cardinal Bernardino Spada, and two very rare terrestrial globes created by the Dutch cartographer, printer, and maker of astronomical instruments, William Blaeu. Signed Caesius, they were crafted in 1622 at Blaeu's Amsterdam printing house, and dedicated to Sweden's Gustav II.

The Spada collection also contains some notable realistic paintings, known as *bambocciate,* (a derisive term linked to the leader of this school of painting, the physically deformed Pieter van Laer). The most gripping of these are by the Roman-born Michelangelo Cerquozzi (1602–1660), notably the *Revolt of Masaniello,* painted in collaboration with the architectural painter Viviano Codazzi.

This dramatic painting illustrates the events of July 7, 1647, when the Neapolitan revolutionary Masaniello (his original name was Tommaso Aniello), led a revolt of the lower classes, burdened by high taxes, against the Spanish rulers of Naples. This uprising was considered serious enough to compel the Spanish viceroy to agree initially to Masaniello's terms, promise to institute reforms, and even recognize him as a general.

Yet, the victory proved short-lived; Masaniello was killed soon after the revolt—either by Spanish agents or his own supporters—and the revolution was repressed.

AN IMPOSING PAINTING OF
THE FEAST OF ANTHONY AND CLEOPATRA
BY FRANCESCO TREVISANI
DOMINATES THIS SECTION
OF THE GALLERY.
IN THE FOREGROUND IS A RARE
SEVENTEENTH-CENTURY DUTCH GLOBE.

Walking through these rooms today, it is impossible not to be awed by the beauty of this collection and the erudition of its former owners, who seem to have been equally at home with the stuccos of the Roman Mannerists, the illusionistic set-pieces of the Baroque, and the realistic themes of the *bambocciate.* And how wonderful for new or returning visitors to stroll through the Spada Palace and Gallery, following in the footsteps of this cultured family, while enjoying their exceptionally diverse collection.

The Villa Farnesina

Via della Lungara, N. 230
Rome 00165
Tel: 06/880–1767

**Open Monday through Saturday
9:00 A.M. to 1:00 P.M.**

Bus: 23, 65, 280

Many visitors to Rome may be unaware that one of the greatest concentrations of High Renaissance art outside the Vatican is preserved inside a splendid villa in Trastevere near the Porta Settimiana. Hidden behind an ivy-covered gate and stone walls, and surrounded by a lush and peaceful garden, where the only sounds are the chirping of birds and the soft splash of a golden marble fountain, the villa was built between 1508 and 1511 by Baldassare Peruzzi (1481–1536) for the great papal banker and arts patron Agostino Chigi.

It is regrettable that one cannot return to the early sixteenth century when Chigi made the Villa Farnesina a gathering-place for his humanist friends, who whiled away the hours

THE LOGGIA OF PSYCHE
IS LOCATED ALONG THE NORTHERN FACADE
OF THE VILLA FARNESINA.

A DETAIL FROM THE ROOM OF THE PERSPECTIVES;
DIANA THE HUNTRESS BY BALDASSARE PERUZZI.

reading classical poetry, discussing philosophy and the finer points of astrology in rooms where the classical myths were brought to life by the leading painters of the day. A renowned and generous host, he delighted in impressing his guests—at one of his banquets he ordered the gold and silver dishes to be tossed into the Tiber after each course was served. In truth, such lavish excess was merely a clever ploy: the businesslike Chigi made sure that nets were concealed at the bottom of the river to catch the precious plate!

Born in Siena in 1466, and heir to an old merchant family whose wealth had been accumulated through commerce and banking, Chigi came to Rome in 1487 and established a bank with a fellow Sienese. Their enterprise soon became so prosperous that other branches were opened in major European cities. The financier went on to acquire land and mines, as well as a port in Tuscany (Porto Ercole), from which his ships sailed the great trade routes of Europe and the East. The Sultan of Turkey dubbed him the "great merchant of Christendom," an appropriate title for a man who loaned money to princes and prelates, and who had business dealings with the kings of Spain, France, and England.

Yet none of his manifold business dealings prevented him from liberally supporting scholars and artists; in 1515, he founded a printing house that published the works of Pindar, the greatest Greek lyric poet, known for his odes celebrating the victors of the Panhellenic games, as well as those of Theocritus, the originator of the pastoral, a poetic form that later was used by Virgil and Spenser.

Not entirely satisfied with his residence on the Via dei Banchi (aptly named the Street of Banks), he purchased several pieces of land across the Tiber and commissioned Peruzzi to build a villa with a magnificent loggia entrance, known as the Loggia of Psyche, opening directly onto the garden. The entire decoration of this magnificent gallery, which was jointly conceived by Peruzzi and Raphael, was intended to give the impression of an open pergola, garlanded with fruit and flowers and shaded by *trompe-l'oeil* "tapestries" painted onto the ceiling. Although it is glazed in today, the loggia was one of the earliest examples of the interpenetration of house and garden, and represents the apogee of the Renaissance villa.

The loggia's frescoes were inspired by a myth from *The Golden Ass* by the second-century Roman satirist, Lucius Apuleius, relating how Psyche'sbeauty was so great that men venerated her more than Venus. To humiliate her rival and avenge herself, the jealous goddess ordered her son Cupid to make the beautiful nymph fall in love with a vile and deformed man. However, Cupid himself became enamored with Psyche as soon as he saw her, and without revealing who he was, took her to his enchanted castle. One night curiosity overcame Psyche and in attempting to discover the identity of her sleeping lover, let a drop of boiling oil fall onto his body, thus forcing the god to awake and flee. Because of Venus's jealousy the nymph was forced to undergo many additional trials, and it was only through the intercession of Jupiter that Psyche was finally reunited with Cupid.

Although Raphael conceived the overall scheme for the loggia, the paintings of Psyche's adventures on the vaults and ceiling are attributed to Francesco Penni and Raffaellino da Colle, as well as to Giulio Romano, Raphael's most talented pupil. The beautiful garlands of botanically accurate fruits, flowers, and vegetables surrounding all these motifs were by Giovanni da Udine, and represent one of the period's finest examples of still-life painting.

That Raphael failed to complete the loggia's decoration for so liberal a patron as Agostino Chigi helped foment a legend that the artist was so distracted by a love affair—presumably with a baker's daughter known as *La Fornarina*—that he neglected his commission. A hundred years after the artist's death, the Chigi Pope Alexander VII (reigned 1655–1667) corroborated this story in a biography of his forebear Agostino. It seems that the delays in Raphael's work, not only at the Chigi villa but also at the Vatican, compelled Leo X to ask Agostino to intercede with the artist on his behalf. The wily banker's solution was to kidnap and hide *La Fornarina*, pretending all the while to Raphael that she had become infatuated with someone else. The stratagem worked only temporarily, however; Raphael grew so melancholy that his work soon slackened. Finally, Chigi was forced to "locate" the object of Raphael's affections and allow her to live with him. (No one knows for certain who was the model for the Psyche series; some think it was *La Fornarina*, while others believe it was Imperia, Chigi's beautiful mistress.)

Raphael did bestir himself to complete one work in the villa—the famous Galatea—in the loggia leading out of the Loggia of Psyche, now called the Room of Galatea. The painting is based on the myth of the sea nymph Galatea, who was loved by Polyphemus, a one-eyed giant, known as the Cyclops. Painted in 1511, between commissions at the Vatican, Raphael's Galatea is an entrancing blend of power and delicacy as she drives her dolphin-led scallop-shell chariot over the waves. The masterfully drawn clumsy giant sitting on a rock looking down longingly at the

THIS CORNER OF THE ROOM
OF THE PERSPECTIVES
BY BALDASSARE PERUZZI
SHOWS A LANDSCAPE WITH A VILLAGE
IN LATIUM FRAMED BY
TROMPE-L'OEIL COLUMNS.

sea nymph (painted by Sebastiano del Piombo, c. 1485–1547, in one of the gallery's lunettes), underscores the drama between the ill-matched pair.

Peruzzi painted the elaborate astrological motifs on the gallery's vault—less well known is that, taken together, they represent the position of the planets at 7:00 P.M., December 1, 1466, the moment of Agostino Chigi's birth.

In the villa's main living room on the second floor of the villa, the visitor is presented with another *tour de force:* the *Salone delle Prospettive* (The Room of Perspectives), one of the earliest Renaissance examples of *trompe-l'oeil* by Peruzzi. Because the artist applied one-point perspective, the real marble floor and its painted counterpart in the frescoes line up from a point between the two doors on the window side of the room.

Between the monumental painted porphyry columns of the simulated loggias at either end of the room, there are charming painted views of Trastevere and the Borgo as they were in the beginning of the sixteenth century. It is still possible to make out such familiar landmarks as the Porta Settimiana, the Teatro di Marcello, the campaniles of Santa Maria in Trastevere and Santo Spirito in Sassia. A series of restorations (which included the removal of a dark reddish brown overpainting executed in the nineteenth century) have not only resulted in the complete recovery of Peruzzi's original decorative scheme, but have also brought to light various sixteenth-century graffiti.

Next to this room is Agostino Chigi's bedroom, where he once had a gold and ivory bed inlaid with precious stones, said to have cost more than the purchase price of the land for his villa. The room's finest frescoes, executed in 1511 by the Sienese painter Il Sodoma (1477–1549), depict scenes from the life of Alexander the Great. Painted at a time when the artist was still smarting with shame at having been superseded by Raphael in the decoration of the Vatican Stanze, the scene of Alexander's

THE WEDDING NIGHT OF ALEXANDER AND ROXANA WAS EXECUTED BY THE SIENESE PAINTER GIOVANNI ANTONIO BAZZI (IL SODOMA).

marriage to Roxana is considered to be Sodoma's masterpiece. While he based the fresco on a famous painting by the Greek artist Aethion described by the Latin author Lucian, he set it in an airy Renaissance bedroom overlooking an adjacent loggia with a sweeping vista.

It is a pity that Sodoma's artistry was not matched by some of the room's other paintings—the representation of Alexander on his white horse, Bucephalus, is certainly not by this artist, although the paintings on either side of it are of his hand. This has led to the supposition that the portrayal of Alexander on his horse was executed by an unknown artist only after Chigi's sumptuous bed had been removed.

After Chigi's death, the villa's famed hospitality and erudite gatherings came to an end. As a result of family quarrels and bad administration, the banker's great fortune was soon dissipated, his treasures sold, and by 1580 the estate had passed into the hands of the Farnese. Hence its current name, thus distinguishing it from the Farnese Palace on the opposite bank of the Tiber, to which it was to have been joined by a bridge. When the new river embankment was built in 1879 not far from Chigi's former estate, an ancient Roman villa was uncovered, revealing splendid painted frescoes and stucco decoration that are now displayed in the Palazzo Massimo alle Terme. It is the sort of find that Chigi, the consummate Renaissance aesthete and humanist, would have greatly appreciated.

The Villa Madama

Monte Mario
Rome 00185
Visits only by pre-arranged
guided tours
with Associazione Città Nascosta.

Tel: 06/331–6059

Metro: Take line A to Ottaviano,
then bus 32 to Via di Villa
Madama.

"CARDINAL Giulio de' Medici, who was afterwards Clement VII, took a site in Rome under Monte Mario where he planned to build a palace with all the comforts and conveniences of apartments, loggias, gardens, fountains, woods, and so forth, the best and most beautiful that could be desired."

This recollection, taken from Giorgio Vasari's *Lives of the Artists,* summarizes one of the most ambitious building projects in sixteenth-century Rome, at a time when the city was being transformed from a backward, underpopulated Medieval town into a city filled with open, airy, and well-lit palaces built and decorated by the leading architects and artists of the Renaissance.

Originally called the "Vigna de' Medici," and now known as the Villa Madama, this elegant edifice remains the only known work of architecture designed by that multifaceted genius, Raphael (1483–1520). In a recently discovered letter, the artist provides a detailed description of this hillside estate, which was intended to replicate the luxurious life of suburban villas in ancient Rome. The original plans called for a luminous triple loggia, a monumental circular court, and rooms designed for large-scale banquets. Foreign dignitaries were to have arrived from the Milvian Bridge (the city's main entrance during the first century B.C.), from which point they would have been invited into a vast terraced garden containing an open-air semicircular theater based on the architecture of other theaters in ancient Rome. With extensive fish ponds and stables capable of holding

A SWEEPING DRIVEWAY LEADS TO THE
ENTRANCE OF VILLA MADAMA;
THE MEDICI COAT-OF-ARMS IS POSTED
ABOVE THE DOOR.

ALTHOUGH CONCEIVED BY RAPHAEL
FOR THE CARDINAL GIULIO DE' MEDICI,
THE LOGGIA'S FRESCOES
WERE PAINTED BY GIULIO ROMANO
AND INTRICATE STUCCOS WERE EXECUTED
BY GIOVANNI DA UDINE.

THE CENTRAL AREA
OF RAPHAEL'S LOGGIA OPENS OUT ONTO
THE "RUSTIC GARDEN,"
WHICH STILL CONTAINS TWO MARRED
STUCCO GIANTS
SCULPTED BY BACCIO BANDINELLI.

up to 400 horses, the estate had been intended to accommodate every imaginable physical and spiritual need. If it had been built according to Raphael's plans, it is likely that it would have been unequaled in all of Italy.

However, the artist's dazzling undertaking was never to be completed. Although Raphael made the first sketches for the villa, Antonio da Sangallo the Younger (who also conceived the celebrated design for the Palazzo Farnese) realized only a fraction of the original designs between 1517 and 1520. The villa's interior decoration was subsequently carried out by Raphael's most talented pupils, Giulio Romano (1499–1546) and Giovanni da Udine (1487–1561). With Raphael's untimely death on April 6, 1520, the two artists soon fell to quarreling, much to the despair of the villa's overseer, Bishop Mario Maffei, who complained of having to work with "two lunatics."

By the summer of 1525, the villa's situation had become perilous. The growing hostility between the powerful Holy Roman Emperor Charles V and Pope Clement VII had culminated in open warfare. Rome was ransacked and pillaged by the Emperor's unpaid and hungry Spanish and Italian mercenaries as well as by German lansquenets, first in September 1526, and then in May 1527. Siding with Charles V, Cardinal Pompeo Colonna attacked the villa himself, while Pope Clement VII, barricaded in Castel Sant' Angelo, wept as he saw smoke rising in the distance from his beloved estate.

After Clement VII's death in 1534, his suburban villa was bequeathed to Duke Alessandro de' Medici. The villa was renamed Villa

Madama, after Alessandro married Margaret of Austria ("Madama"), the natural daughter of Charles V, who also gave her name to the headquarters of the Italian Senate, Palazzo Madama. Born in Flanders in 1522, the illegitimate child of the Hapsburg Emperor and the daughter of a Flemish tapestry manufacturer, Margaret had been educated at the princely court of her great-aunt Margaret, daughter of Maximilian of Austria and the ruler of the Netherlands. Widowed at fifteen, Margaret was remarried (much against her will), to Pope Paul III's nephew Ottavio Farnese, so that upon her death the estate reverted to the Farnese family.

With the subsequent decline and disappearance of the Farnese family, followed by the Napoleonic occupation of Rome and the establishment of the Kingdom of Italy, the villa was robbed of its artistic furnishings and suffered significant damage. In 1916, the Florentine newspaper *Il Marzocco* reported: "Of this palace which was one of the most beautiful and singular landmarks of the Renaissance, built by Raphael and most perfectly decorated by his pupils, only a house without doors and windows is left, exposed to the rain and wind, having lost much of its inside and outside decorations. Until some years ago it was used as a hay-loft."

Touring the handsomely restored Villa Madama today (now used by the Italian Foreign Office for entertainments during state visits), one cannot help but be moved by the painstaking efforts that have been taken to save the edifice from further decay. While most of the credit must go to Count Carlo Dentice di Frasso and his American wife, Dorothy Cadwell Taylor, who restored the villa from 1925 to 1928, one should not forget Maurice Bergés, an industrial engineer from Toulouse who spent most of his personal fortune trying to rescue the villa, before being forced to sell it to Count Dentice di Frasso a year prior to his death.

Villa Madama's most breathtaking feature is Raphael's impressive loggia, which is divided into three bays and closed over by barrel vaults, that were meant to replicate the same spatial relationships found in ancient Roman baths. Scholars believe the loggia's dazzling frescoes of grotesques and stucco-work, executed respectively by Giulio Romano and Giovanni da Udine, were inspired by the discovery in 1517 of Nero's Golden House, also known as the *Domus Aurea*.

Unfortunately, only a fraction of this painted decor is now visible. All the lower part of the loggia, which was once covered with grotesques from the hand of da Udine, was damaged and effaced by the ravages of warfare and weather at a time when the loggia's outer arcades were not protected by glass doors as they are today. Nonetheless, one can still admire the ceiling decorations, which pay tribute to the fantastic pagan world that the Italian humanists were rediscovering through Ovid's tales in the *Metamorphoses*. In the loggia's central vault, around the Medici coat of arms, the artists chose to personify the Four Seasons and intersperse them with mythological scenes featuring the figures of Jupiter, Juno, Neptune, Pluto, and Proserpine.

In the cross-vault and corresponding apse unfolds the tragic love story of Polyphemus, the god of sleep, who slays Galatea's beloved shepherd boy Acis with a stone in a fit of jealous rage. This is the very painting that Vasari acclaims in his writing on Romano: "Giulio painted in fresco a huge Polyphemus with innumerable children and little satyrs playing round him, for which he won great

THE BRONZE DOOR KNOCKERS
WITH LION HEADS
ARE MODELED AFTER THOSE THAT WERE
USED IN THE ORIGINAL CONSTRUCTION
OF VILLA MADAMA.

THE VAULTED CEILING
OF THIS VAST ROOM FEATURES,
IN THE CENTRAL PANEL,
THE CARDINAL'S COAT OF ARMS,
SURROUNDED BY A COLORED STUCCO GARLAND
OF FLOWERS AND FRUIT,
AND ORNAMENTED BY THE SUN AND THE MOON.
THE SMALLER PANELS
ALTERNATE FIGURES OF POETS
WITH DANCING GIRLS AND EXOTIC ANIMALS,
SIMILAR TO THOSE
THAT WERE KEPT IN LEO X'S SMALL ZOO
AT THE BELVEDERE.

praise, as he did for all the works and designs he executed for that place."

The Medici emblems are featured prominently in the loggia's vaulting: one depicts a lion's head and a radiant sun; another a falcon grasping a diamond ring, the symbol of undaunted pride; another contains three feathers in white, red, and green and the motto *semper* ("always," alluding to the family's motto of faith, hope, and charity); while another displays a seal of a sun with the motto *soave*, alluding to the family's suave and urbane government of Florence.

Standing out among them all is Giulio de' Medici's personal crest of sunrays piercing a crystal globe and setting fire to a stump with the Latin motto *Candor illesus* ("I burn and remain unburnt")—hardly prophetic in light of the villa's destruction during the Sack of Rome.

Next to Raphael's loggia is the other masterpiece of Villa Madama—a reception room that is now referred to as Giulio Romano's Hall, since that artist was responsible for most of the wall and ceiling decorations. The ceiling's large central panel displays the Cardinal's coat of arms surrounded by a colored stucco garland of flowers and fruit and enhanced by representations of Diana and Apollo, while the smaller panels represent different arts, as well as such exotic animals as the emu, the ostrich, and the turkey, all of which were kept in the Vatican's private zoo.

A visit to this villa also offers an opportunity to take in some of the loveliest views of Rome, as well as to discover two classic Renaissance gardens. The loggia leads out toward an Italian formal garden composed of geometrically-shaped plantings of fragrant boxwood, and framed by a triple arcade divided by pillars, which was designed by Raphael.

Da Udine created this garden's famed Elephant Fountain in a mosaic-embellished vault, whose nautical motif is derived from an ancient Roman *nymphaeum*. The animal's head is believed to be a portrait of the famous Indian elephant Annone (the ancient name for Carthage), brought to Rome by a Portuguese delegation from Goa, India, in 1514, which soon became the favorite pet of Leo X and the Roman populace. Upon the elephant's death, the Pope even ordered Raphael to design a tomb for the fabled pachyderm. (It was later destroyed.)

Visitors will be charmed to see the fountain's waters springing from the elephant's trunk, only to reappear in a rectangular turquoise-colored pool embellished by two bronze Farnese lilies at the edge of the garden's terrace, and then once again in the monumental fish pond beneath the terrace where the Cardinal and his guests used to fish during the summer months.

Two very weathered stucco giants sculpted by Baccio Bandinelli (1488–1560) lead us through the gates of the Italian formal garden into a rustic garden composed of thickets and rows of poplars, rock formations, and *nymphaea*, as well as a row of ancient columns that once held the busts of Roman emperors. It is easy to imagine how the shaded paths of this garden once gave Cardinal Giulio de' Medici and his guests hours of delicious respite from Rome's summer heat and political turmoil. Those of us who have a chance to see it today, can rejoice in knowing that this architectural masterpiece was able to extend its triumph over the brutalities of warfare, and thus preserve for the present visitor a site that is one of the unique treasures of the Renaissance in Rome.

BIBLIOGRAPHY

———◆———

Bazin, Germain.
Baroque and Rococo
London: Thames and Hudson, 1993.

Belford, Ros.
The Virago Woman's Travel Guide
Berkeley, California: Ulysses Press, 1993.

Bertoletti, Marina; Cima, Maddalena; and Emilia Talamo.
Sculptures of Ancient Rome, Collections from the Capitoline Museums at the Montemartini Power Station.
Milan: Electa, 1997.

Capon, Laura.
Il Museo Napoleonico
Rome: Fratelli Palombi, S.r.l.

Carcopino, Jérôme.
Daily Life in Ancient Rome
London: Penguin Books, Ltd., 1991.

Carr-Gomm, Sarah.
Rome: Art in Focus
London: Studio Editions Ltd., 1995.

Catalli, Fiorenzo, and Petrecca, Mauro
Villa Pamphilj
Rome: Istituto Poligrafico e Zecca dello Stato, 1992.

Colantunono, Patrizio, Editor.
Anzio: Cartoline illustrate dal 1900 al 1945
Rome: Outline, 1995.

D'Ambra, Eve.
Roman Art
Cambridge: Cambridge University Press, 1998.

Davies, Norman.
Europe: A History
London: Pimlico (Random House), 1997.

De Chirico, Giorgio.
Mémoires.
Paris: La Table Ronde, 1965.

De Santi, Floriano (Editor).
Museo Donazione Umberto Mastroianni
Rome: Il Cigno Galileo Galilei Edizioni Di Arte E Scienza, 1995.

Ferraris, Patrizia Rosazza.
Il Museo Praz
Rome: Edizioni SACS, 1996.

Franchi, Luisa dell'Orto.
Ancient Rome: Life and Art
Rome: Scala, 1982.

Geller, Ruth Liliana.
Jewish Rome, A Pictorial History of 2000 Years
Rome: Viella S.R.L., 1984.

Gerlini, Elsa.
Villa Farnesina alla Lungara, Rome
Rome: Istituto Poligrafico e Zecca Dello Stato, 1990.

Gombrich, E. H.
The Story of Art
London: Phaidon Press Ltd., 1995.

Guhl, E., and Koner, W.
The Romans: Their Life and Customs
Twickenham, Middlesex: Senate (Tiger Books International plc), 1994.

Harris, William H., and Levey, Judith S. (Editors)
The New Columbia Encyclopedia
New York and London: Columbia University Press, 1975.

Haskell, Francis.
Patrons and Painters
New Haven and London: Yale University Press, 1980.

Hughes, Robert.
Nothing If Not Critical
New York: Penguin Books, 1990.

Lentz, Thierry.
Napoléon "Mon ambition était grande"
Paris: Gallimard, 1998.

Macadam, Alta.
Rome: Blue Guide
London: A & C Black (Publishers) Ltd., 1998.

Mantovano, Paola, and Appolloni Cristiana.
Storie di Ruote
Rome: Poolgrafica, 1998.

Masson, Georgina.
The Companion Guide to Rome
Bungay, Suffolk: The Chaucer Press,
Ltd., 1972.

Moatti, Claude.
The Search for Ancient Rome
London: Thames & Hudson, 1993.

Morton, H. V.
A Traveller in Rome
London: Methuen & Co., Ltd., 1960.

Murray, Peter and Linda.
Penguin Dictionary of Art and Artists
London: Penguin Books Ltd., 1997.

Praz, Mario.
Histoire de la Décoration d'Intérieur
Paris: Thames & Hudson SARL, 1994.

Procacci, Giuliano.
History of the Italian People
London: Penguin Books, 1991.

Recupero, Jacopo.
The Farnese Palace at Caprarola.
Florence: Bonechi Edizioni Il Turismo,
1975.

Rewald, John.
Giacomo Manzù
London: Thames & Hudson, 1967.

Santi, Maresita Nota, and Cimino,
Maria Gabriella.
Barracco Museum Rome
Rome: Istituto Poligrafico e Zecca Dello
Stato, 1993.

Scoppola, Francesco, and Vordemann,
Stella Diana.
Palazzo Altemps
Milan: Electa, 1997.

Servi, Sandro.
The Jewish Museum of Rome
Florence: Arti Grafiche Alinari Baglioni,
S.p.A., 1985.

Settis, Salvatore, Editor; Texts by
Bonamici, Maria; Francovich,
Riccardo; Cremonesi, Renata Grifoni;
Ricci, Andreina; Rombai, Leonardo.
The Land of the Etruscans
Milano: Scala, 1985.

Silverio, Anna Maria Liberati.
Museo della Civilta Romana
Rome: Edizioni Latium, 1988.

Tagliamonte, Gianluca.
Baths of Diocletian
Milan: Electa, 1998.

Tulard, Jean; Gengembre, Gérard;
Goetz, Adrien; Jourquin, Jacques;
and Lentz, Thierry.
L'ABCdaire de Napoléon et de l'Empire
Paris: Flammarion, 1998.

Vasari, Giorgio (Translated by George
Bull).
Lives of the Artists, Volume I and Volume II.
London: Penguin Books, 1987.

Vicini, Maria Lucrezia.
Galleria Spada: Visita Guidata
Rome: Rotostampa S.r.l., 1997.

Visentini, Margherita Azzi; Boitani,
Francesca; Proietti, Giuseppe; Rizzo,
M. Antonietta.
Villa Giulia Museum
Milan: Leonardo Arte S.R.L., 1992.

Visser, Margaret.
Much Depends on Dinner.
New York: Collier Books, 1988.

Wheeler, Sir Mortimer.
Roman Art and Architecture.
London: Thames and Hudson, 1996.

Wölfflin, Heinrich
Renaissance and Baroque
Ithaca, New York: Cornell University
Press, 1992.

INDEX

◆